ADOPTION RECKONINGS

ADOPTION RECKONINGS

FOR THREE REFRIGERATORS AND A WASHING MACHINE

GONDA VAN STEEN

ANTHEM PRESS

Anthem Press
An imprint of Wimbledon Publishing Company
www.anthempress.com

This edition first published in UK and USA 2025
by ANTHEM PRESS
75–76 Blackfriars Road, London SE1 8HA, UK
or PO Box 9779, London SW19 7ZG, UK
and
244 Madison Ave #116, New York, NY 10016, USA

British Library Cataloguing-in-Publication Data
A catalogue record for this book is available from the British Library.

Library of Congress Cataloging-in-Publication Data: 2025934729
A catalog record for this book has been requested.

ISBN-13: 978-1-83999-503-3 (Pbk)
ISBN-10: 1-83999-503-3 (Pbk)

Credit: Gonda Van Steen

This title is also available as an eBook.

Dedicated to the many Greek adoptees who were willing to share their experiences, and to many more whose stories remain untold.

CONTENTS

LIST OF FIGURES

FOREWORD

The lengthy essay of Part I contextualizes the first edition of the play, called *For Three Refrigerators and a Washing Machine*, and offers an introduction focused on history, theory, and praxis. This introduction discusses how and why a collectively written playscript on the historic adoptions from postwar Greece came about. After historical analysis, it was time for the adopted persons' voices to be heard more clearly. It was time also to try a life-writing project that would be about learning as well as sharing, first with other adoptees, then with theater audiences, by way of bringing a new playscript to the stage. Part I presents the innovative playscript of Part II as the product of a collective life-writing and composition process. It explains how the script organically grew into an example of a "verbatim" theater experiment, or "testimony theater," as it has been rediscovered recently. Thus, combining history (archival and oral) and creative nonfiction writing, the play *For Three Refrigerators and a Washing Machine* opens pathways for readers (and viewers) to comprehend life histories shaped by adoption from "poorer" countries and stories subjugated by early Cold War geopolitics.

ACKNOWLEDGMENTS

I express my abiding gratitude to all my King's College London co-workers and students, who have been following this unusual book project through its various stages of—slow—progression. In mid-March of 2020, King's sent nearly all its staff home to start working remotely. The coronavirus (COVID-19) outbreak forced different conditions onto everyone. London was preparing for a massive lockdown. With the support of colleagues and friends, with whom we formed a quaran-team, I buckled down for long months of staying indoors. Academics idealize long, uninterrupted spans of quiet time to read and write, but the pandemic ushered in an era of taxing circumstances. Despite the havoc, I rediscovered the productive power of life-writing and the boldness that life-changing conditions can ignite. The reactions to the pandemic made me think hard about many issues and reoriented me toward others. This study "enfleshes" those recent crisis conditions, and it feels emboldened to speak out about older, life-impacting predicaments.

The heartfelt acknowledgments that I expressed in my 2019 book still stand, and this study, too, builds on the help offered by many in prior years. I am obliged to many more people for the engaged conversations we had since on the topic of postwar and Cold War adoptions: Yiorgos Anagnostou, Efi Avdela, Maria Bouri, Stratis Bournazos, Eleni Bozia, Aigli Brouskou, Mary Cardaras, Atamhi Cawayu, Elpida Chochliourou, Konstantinos Daskalou, Nikiforos Diamandouros, Rosemary Donnelly, Gabrielle Glaser, John O. Iatrides, Spyros Kakouriotis, Vangelis Karamanolakis, Katerina Karra, Ghassan Khalil, Alexander Kitroeff, Artemis Kliafa, Gregory Kontos, Triantafyllos Kotopoulos, Dimitra Lampropoulou, Anna Mavroleon, John McLeod, George I. Paganelis, Hari Prasad Sacré, Niall Sreenan, Niki Troullinou, and John Zervos. Clare Brant, then-codirector of King's Centre for Life-Writing Research, extended useful advice on how to frame the bigger questions in light of the demands of life-writing as a research field and publication area. Elias Malandris lent his eager ear and then kindly provided support with the anticipated play production on site in Athens.

The very professional archivists and especially Amalia Pappa and Anna Koulikourdi at the General State Archives in Athens generously assisted me on my many visits and return visits. Equally helpful was Linnea Anderson, archivist at the Social Welfare History Archives of the Elmer L. Andersen Library at the University of Minnesota. The discreet practical assistance of Panagiotis Adamopoulos, Olympia Anastasopoulou, Aphrodite Bouikidis, Riya Mavroidis, and Peter Swallow was unrelenting, as was their friendship. Kalli Karveli of the Hellenic Data Protection Authority inspired me to think hard about the ethics of utilizing-by-anonymizing any personal information.

Interested academic audiences in the United States, the United Kingdom, and in Greece, especially, kept delivering opinions, comments, and questions long after the dates of my various lectures had passed. I thank Liana Giannakopoulou and the Society for Modern Greek Studies, who invited me to present at the London Hellenic Centre; Eustathia Papadodima, who asked me to deliver a research seminar at the Academy of Athens; and Ianthi Tsimpli and Tim Whitmarsh, who included my lecture in the Greek Dialogues series, organized by the Cambridge Centre for Greek Studies and the Cambridge Hellenic Learned Society at Cambridge University. Elsa Amanatidou and Vangelis Calotychos kindly hosted an online interview about the topic of the Greek-to-American adoption history. Through its then-new "Zoom" format, the interview opened up the conversation with virtual attendees from far and wide and also allowed many of the adoptees themselves to participate. More online presentations followed during the many months of the Covid-19 pandemic restrictions and through its aftermath. Their audiences posed questions that sharpened not only my thoughts but also my priorities. In 2023, the American College of Greece invited me to deliver the 27th Kimon Friar Lecture, on "Child Adoption: Greek Myth, Literature, and Reality," and extended fabulous hospitality. While preparing for these presentations, the support of Alex Kalamarides, Ilias Katsos, Anna Kyriakidou, Michael Sanidas, and Niki Trouillinou has been an added and much-valued bonus. Also, Anastasia Lambria and Kostas Papadopoulos from Potamos Publishers offered translation and publication advice when it was most needed. I have rarely felt so supported by any publishing house as I am by Potamos. Journalists Katerina Bakogianni, Petros Diplas, Nikos Konstandaras, Dimitris Kontogiannis, Niki Lymberaki, and Margarita Pournara created new momentum, each in their own way. I am grateful also to my current, incisive editors and to Golda Merline and Jebaslin Hephzibah, for their enthusiasm and professionalism. I am much obliged also to the anonymous readers of an earlier version of the full book manuscript, for keeping focused on delivering the best possible product. I remain indebted to the reviewers of my 2019 book, who left excellent advice to apply to this one. I must accept full responsibility for this book's shortcomings: its faults are mine, but all of the above contributors have made them fewer in number.

The Greek-born adoptees have welcomed me as an "insider," with the most profound trust and reciprocity, for which I am immensely grateful. I deeply admire and value their willingness to revisit disquieting aspects of their lives in honest discussion and writing. They have improved the quality of this playscript and study by asking questions and raising occasional objections. They have made the experience of researching and writing more rewarding. But most of all, their histories have had a profound impact on me, and I hope that they will also influence others in life-altering ways. Therefore, I once again thank the many Greek adoptees who have been central to this and the previous book and articles, those whom I have interviewed or with whom I have otherwise communicated, who offered up private records for review, who wrote about their experiences, who met with me at reunions, and who have followed my work with keen interest. I thank all of them, but especially those who have joined me in digging deeper into tough truths: Alex, Alexis, Andrew, Chrisy, Diana, Dinos, Effie, Elaine, Ellen, Evi, Fran, Karin, Ken, Lori, Maria, Marie, Markella, Michael, Mindy, Nick, Pamela, Paula, Penny, Petros, Robert, Robyn, Rick, Stephanie, Theodora, Tommy, and Zoe. A warm and humble thank-you goes to those adoptees who have patiently shared their full stories, which, to me, appreciated in value over time. They also gave me permission to use their social media posts, personal emails, blogs, or songs, to which they generously directed me. Maria Heckinger let me use her photographs on numerous occasions. I hope that even those whose literal words or whose pictures did not make it into this book can see still something of themselves reflected. All adoptees and interlocutors also kindly consented to the use of the variety of data on which this book draws—in fact, they have only ever embraced the research and writing initiatives that have brought visibility to their collective history. I look up to people like the Greek adoptees and the vocal adoptee activists (especially Mary Cardaras at The Demos Center, Gregory Luce, and David Smolin), who have the courage to report wrongdoing and claim their right. The investigative study and writing process in which I have engaged often proves to be no more than a short sprint in the marathon that they have been running for years.

My close collaboration with Israeli documentary filmmaker Ronit Kertsner gave my life-writing project a new impetus at the right time. She, Shalom Rufeisen, and several now-friends among the intercountry adoptees of diverse origins have made multiple contributions to the visual and cross-cultural expansion of the writing process. We lost Ronit on September 24, 2020, but we remember her as a force of life with a keen intellect and an even sharper wit.

She pulled us together even after her death, and we will realize her wish to see her last documentary film, *The Greek Connection*, completed.

A very special thank-you goes to the talented stage practitioners of Culture in Action and in particular to Kyriaki Mitsou, who was the driving force behind the initiative to turn Greek adoption-related testimonies into a playscript for broad audiences eager to learn about this forgotten part of postwar history. With Renata Sofrona and Romina Spyraki, Kyriaki took care to shape the play production derived from the original script into the best possible version of itself. All three of them also helped me to make contacts among theater practitioners and artists through the very effective snowball method. There is no stopping three committed individuals like them, who have only quality and commitment at heart. Additionally, I thank Jasmine Newton-Rae and Ellen Scott-Smith for lending their sharp eye and fine ear during rehearsals, as we nervously built up to the October 24, 2024 London premiere of the play. Incubated in the company of these remarkable people and supported by a fabulous cast and crew, the play won acclaim in the United Kingdom and has now been invited to venues across Greece. I have listened respectfully to postproduction viewpoints that may not be in line with my own or with those of the stage producer and actors. We acknowledge the significant personal insights that attendees and critics have shared. I continue to try to be faithful to the essence of their perspectives. Funding from the Arts Council England and the Schilizzi Foundation Social History Workshops created the encouragement as well as the space to experiment with writing in new ways and for new audiences. I value the foundation's consistent support for topics that explore Greece's social and family history. Like no other, Maria Heckinger and Stephanie Pazoles understood the emotional labor—and occasional drain—that went into this kind of community-based process, its demands of organizing and advocacy work.

The influence of my husband, Greg Terzian, runs deep in these pages. As is his habit, he contributes in ways that make a big—and loving—difference. I dedicate this book to Eleni Bozia. She showed me how much one can do in just one lifetime, and how important it is to engage one's lifetime with a positive attitude, with love and support. I wish strength to all those whose lives have been upended, who were left to pick up the pieces and move on. As we continue to navigate the ever-changing landscape created by the recent pandemic, we are slowly building a new "normal." I am reminded of all the cross-border adoptees who had to do just that, who had to make new lives work for them, without staying connected to anything they had known before. From a very early age, they confronted the question of what makes people who they are, head-on. They have been so generous with the much-needed answers. Thank you!

PART I

INTRODUCTION: *ADOPTION RECKONINGS*: RAW WRITING ABOUT POSTWAR INTERNATIONAL ADOPTION

Preface

She shows a great deal of interest in all around her, grasps a pencil and tries to put it in her mouth, and follows moving objects with her eyes. Alert. Greek.
(Quoted from the adoption papers of Greek adoptee K., December 1956)

Adoption is an ambivalent, emotionally resonant, and never-finished issue. This essay offers a different approach to a complex matter. It is not a head-on analysis; it is, rather, a two-pronged approach: one an introduction, the second an edited playscript in the form of "testimony theater," titled *For Three Refrigerators and a Washing Machine* (hereafter *FTRWM*).[1] Together, they engage with the details of a case study of postwar and Cold War international adoption: the "historic" adoptions from Greece to the United States are presented here in a "verbatim" format, in which all parties related to this adoption movement will have their say. As the introduction to this playscript will explain, this "verbatim" theater experiment may at first look like an assemblage, but tones and trends soon become discernable. Thus, the play acquires a documentary value that transforms readers into spectators, then into eyewitnesses. But how did we get here? And why do the Greek "historic" adoptions, which are anything but "historic," have something important to share with you?

In *Adoption, Memory, and Cold War Greece* (2019), I placed the lens of international child adoption on a new analysis of the Civil War and Cold War periods in modern Greek history and in Greek-American relations. I also showed how

1

postwar Greece "invented" the template for international adoption as we now know it. My research has been campaign-based as well as source-based since 2013, when I first set out on this path. This edition of the play *FTRWM* is the product of my lengthy involvement with adopted persons but also with larger communities of readers, educators, expectant mothers, genetic counselors, medical and other practitioners, and lawyers and activists. I have come to conclude that postwar international adoption from Greece was, in the end, unfair to all parties, including the adoptive parents, who were left in the dark and occasionally even deceived. "Good" international adoption is an extremely difficult ideal to achieve—if not impossible—even under the current conditions, let alone under the past acute circumstances of political and socioeconomic disparity and dependency. To this day, quasi-colonial and neocolonial relations of exploitation make international adoptions very problematic (and leave them vulnerable to abuse), even if the first parents of the "adoptable" child have registered (notional) informed consent. Additionally, the acute sense of a cultural as well as a genetic dislocation is significant for the adopted person, who is often silenced when voicing legitimate concerns about the psychological cost of adoption. Well-conceived policy interventions, which should be context-specific, ought to be considered to address such issues; some interventions may be or may fall short of an outright ban.

Let's just clear the air about international adoption immediately and hopefully start a constructive dialogue. I have not adopted. I am not adopted, although ... Where do I come from? Where do I stand then? How do I approach the relatively new field of adoption history and study? Since 2013, I can call myself adoption-conscious or "adoption-informed" at best. I look critically at cross-border adoptions of the earliest waves, which have been—paradoxically—ever-dynamic. International adoption, then and now, is far from representing an absolute, unmitigated good. It is not an ideologically benign practice. I do not approve of the public's and the media's love affair with international adoption, in which the past is sanitized and emotions are kept at a safe distance. The adoption industry has long romanticized images of adopted children, and it has facilitated the romanticizing of adoption from abroad, especially. Such representations barely touch on the realities that adoptees themselves have lived. They dismiss the adoptees' own cautionary tales. Adoption requires honest analysis rather than reverie.

I aim to offer a different, performative, and life-course perspective on child adoption from Greece without shaming anyone who has found himself or herself persuaded by the adoption industry's relentless propaganda. Books by adopters and practitioners have been written, reams of them. The voices of the adoptees themselves have only just begun to be heard—and to be taken seriously. By presenting the play *FTRWM* based on Greek adoptees and other voices, I pursue an open-ended engagement with the state of being adopted—then and now. Personally, and from a mid-2020s perspective, I view international adoption as a twentieth-century social experiment that has long run its course, that brought some good to some children in need, but that did damage to many more people (beyond the adopted persons), and that left thousands of adoptees without legal options or other support in later life. International adoption is past due, and it is time to learn from mistakes made and to do so based on the input of those who have lived adoption. It is time to flip the script on the image of adoption as a social good without any downsides. For too many adoptees, the new family was not a refuge but a perennial emotional minefield. For too many first families, the adoption of their child or sibling was the beginning of a life of invisible, unvoiced grief. Admittedly, failure to parent exists among biological parents just as it exists among adoptive parents, and we hope the cases are as rare as possible. Without entering into a binary framework of adoptees as victims and adopters as perpetrators, this edition presents an opportunity, rather, to break the codes of silence. An opportunity to do some myth-busting about adoption, not just to destroy but to add new perspectives and to demand new solutions. The playscript that follows, then, must account for the other side of the argument and must challenge adoption as a given or default option. Within the purview of child welfare, in which adoption has often been taken for granted, we must ask why adoption and why adoption in its current and past forms. Can the proposition of sending children to the other end of the world be meaningfully valid? Has it ever been? We must question the very premise of cut-tie and cut-throat adoption and the persistent tacit acceptance of it.

Since 2013, I have studied the post-WWII and Cold War adoptions of Greek-born children sent to the United States and the Netherlands in close communication with many of those who were—and therefore still are—adopted. In the postwar mindset, the US-bound adoption of Greek children constituted another form of humanitarian "aid" to Greece, war-torn and destitute. It also discouraged the Greek state from creating or strengthening local social and family welfare networks. The experiences of the Greek adoptees sent to the States, especially of those dispatched at an older age (up to age fourteen), have been very mixed; some have been nothing short of traumatic. My interaction with this forgotten group of adoptees has left me convinced that international adoption should not happen at the speed it did then and at the cost it does now. I do not discount the efforts of well-meaning parties, but I do wish for the children in need of adult care not to be uprooted, but to remain, rather, in the care of their families or of other close, healthy, and safe relatives, in their native countries—as close as possible to their origins. I speak of children needing families, not of families needing children. Only in extreme circumstances can international adoption become justifiable, if and when all other domestic solutions or alternatives have been thoroughly exhausted. International adoption places too much distance between the biological family and the adoptive family, foreclosing the possibility of the child ever returning to the former or of entering into a kinship placement. A strong, sound foster system, on the other hand, is part of a solid continuum of care and must lift the binary of adopting out or not. The same holds true for forms of legal guardianship or long-term care orders, which do not erase the child's prior identity and do not "amend" (or "disappear") birth certificates. These and other in-between solutions must keep focused on strengthening the first families in the hope of returning the children to their parents, siblings, grandparents, or other close relatives. Prolonged institutional care is not a solution that I support, either, since it lessens the incentives to reunite children with their loved ones. International adoption, however, remains an unnecessarily drastic solution to what may be a short-term crisis. The need for psychologically responsible solutions has traditionally been great, as is the need for ethical placements, not just legal placements. The bottom line is, "the best interest of the child" is an adult invention, and a Western, heteronormative, white middle-class, and nuclear-family-exclusive construct at that. Adoption is a choice for adoptive parents, but it is not a choice for the adoptee. A child should not be sought, or acquired, to fulfill the rights and wishes of adults desiring to parent. Where does the right to a child leave the rights of the child? Given the shifting historical perspectives on "the best interest of the child," what exactly does this overused phrase mean in the 2020s?[2]

For the past seven and a half decades, the typical far-flung adoption "for the child's own good" has proven to be the ultimate path of no return. The legal incorporation into a new family and the routine lack of proper oversight and follow-up have generated plenty of unhappy circumstances associated with the kind of permanent, irreversible displacement that could and should have been avoided. Any adoption's successful outcome cannot depend on the "luck" of the child but must be the result of the hard work of the adoptive parents, both before and after the adoption takes place. The random kindness of random strangers should not be the defining factor of a "successful" adoption. US-bound adoptions from Greece did help some children, but almost accidentally so. Such "lucky" strikes do not justify, let alone exonerate, the old system, and they detract from the abuses that did take place. Reunions later in life do not erase the prior circumstances for delivering a "happy end"—they are only the beginning of more hard work on the part of the adopted persons. Professional and competent services should be available to assist with the aftercare, especially, and be prepared for the *longue durée*.

Meanwhile, adult adoptees are (rightfully) upset to still see people swoon over foreign adoptees while balking at the release of embarrassing statistics or other news, cursory home studies, illegal practices, and so on, which taint adoptions to this day. New adoption scandals erupt every so often, and they unmask new players using the same old tactics. To their credit, some adoptive parents and even former mediators are at the forefront of the fight against illicit adoption practices. Scores of adoptive parents fiercely love their adopted children, and helping them search and advocate can be fulfilling for all involved: who would want to stand in the way of adopted persons learning about their medical history and being able to take preventive steps to extend their anticipated lifespan? Other adoptive parents deliver their best efforts; some, nonetheless, fail. Many are so committed to the project of parenting that they forget to come up for air and reflect. All of them, too, are hamstrung by the dominant adoption narrative of "happily ever after," which prevents many from seeking help when challenges present themselves. Nancy Verrier, author of *The Primal Wound* (1993) and an adoptive parent herself, noted: "[L]ove and devotion can only go so far in annulling [the child's sense of] loss, even if—especially if—it is not verbalized."[3] Even in the best-case scenario of a child adopted into a loving family, loss is still a pervasive feeling that must be fully acknowledged. This edition is, therefore, not an indictment of adoptive parents, some of whom rise above their own needs and invest endless amounts of time and care, with sensitivity to the issues raised by adoption. This play is not anti-adoption. The challenge is not to ask if one is "with" or "against" adoption but to understand how adoption happened and why, how it came to be taken for granted, and what effects it has left behind. The play further asks, however, how adoptees came to be de-voiced, and it demonstrates that their voices can be restored, if only belatedly. Thus, the challenge has been to shift the focus from the explanations given by adopters and agents or mediators to the impact of adoption, to which the adoptees themselves will attest. This edition is just making sure that the least-heard voices in adoptions finally receive their turn, that the unsaid parts of international adoption, especially, can finally be spoken.

Such ideas as those expressed above would have struck the authorities of postwar Greece as anachronistically "modern" and demanding, as out-of-touch with the harsh realities on the ground. The US-bound adoption flow was seen as a means for Greece to emerge from and transcend the divisive history and economic destruction of the 1940s. Adoptions could not move fast enough. They were met by America's insatiable demand for adoptable children in the era of the so-called "white baby shortage." The notion of aftercare barely existed, and many of its current practices were not deemed necessary. After all, the children's "happier" life began with their arrival in the United States, following their "rescue" from poverty, neglect, and other dire circumstances. And doesn't parental love conquer all? There has been far more naiveté than truth to such statements, and the growing adoption-critical movement is making its case loud and clear. Also, let's make sure to add awareness, respect, dedication, and endless patience to that parental love that must conquer all. Adoption delivers a tall order to everyone involved, but most of all to the adopted person.

This opening salvo may come as a shock to some readers. Let me explain why and how we need to drill down to the hard truth. Some 4,000 Greek children were moved for adoption to the United States between 1948 and 1975. Another 600 Greek children were adopted out to the Netherlands. The fate of the hundreds of Greek-born children who were adopted out overseas has only recently received attention, but prior to 2019, not even their number was firmly established. The Greek state of the postwar decades failed to collect the adoption-related data, and researchers were hampered also by the long-guarded confidentiality surrounding adoption procedures and files. My research has debunked two stubborn misperceptions for the Greek public and local officials: 1) that the mass overseas adoptions of Greek children *never* happened; 2) that these adoptions ran into the tens of thousands. These misperceptions could not be more contradictory. The majority of those 4,000 Greek children passed through independent adoption schemes or private handlers, while licensed agencies such as the International Social Service (ISS) undertook fewer cases. Some charitable yet entrepreneurial organizations, such as the very visible American Hellenic Educational Progressive Association (AHEPA), handled a large number of cases without the input of child experts or welfare professionals but with enough legal expertise to ultimately steer clear of Greek or American procedural roadblocks—a few scandals notwithstanding.[4] Some self-anointed "child-savers" ventured out on their own in the new, uncharted territory of Greek adoptions abroad. Private lawyers and other middlemen managed to stay somewhat under the radar by focusing on relatively small geographical areas or on specific (ethnic) clienteles with which to place children from Greece. Thus, Father Spyridon (Spyros) Diavatis catered to southern Texas, whereas Maurice and Rebecca Issachar courted childless New York Jewish couples. Licensed agencies, on the other hand, tried hard to keep the opportunists in check, or at least to keep them more honest. They adhered to more modern and nonsectarian principles, but they still guided children toward overseas and permanent adoption as the supposedly only alternative to institutional care. However, these agencies could not but disappoint prospective parents with their longer waiting periods and more complex procedures, which many American parents deemed unnecessary, especially if they already enjoyed the approval of their ethnic, religious, or class communities. Thus, the postwar Greek adoption landscape was one, not of coordination, but of fierce competition—a phenomenon still prevalent in modern theaters of international adoption—and, if anything, of declining rather than increasing professionalization through the 1950s. Some US-bound adoptions proved to be illegal or illicit. Many of them could have been and ought to have been prevented altogether if both the sending country and the main recipient, the United States, had been willing to examine and invest in other options, such as strengthening a social welfare network supportive of young unmarried women. But even the mothers' shelter founded by the Greek Queen Frederica, the Babies' Center Mitera (1955), steered vulnerable, unwed young women in the direction of the only "suitable" plan, that of adoption.[5] The prospect of returning the Greek-born child to a single birth parent or other birth relatives was often not viable or not politically desirable (given the prevalent anticommunist prejudice that targeted leftist families for years). Long-term institutional care was costly, but it also tied older children, especially, to the Greek royalist or conservative institutions that, by the early 1950s, had established a nationwide monopoly on such care. Far too many Greek adoptions were based on the adoption-by-proxy system, which took advantage of the vulnerabilities of first mothers and destitute families, who, if granted even a modest measure of assistance, would have kept their children.

Hundreds of Greek-born adoptees today bear the consequences—and some bear the actual scars—of an adoption movement that did not seek alternative or even delayed solutions, that enriched the middlemen of a child export circuit, and that was then silenced for some seventy years. Greece often thought of international adoption as the first, not as the last solution, and as the only solution. If children really needed to be sent abroad, the procedures should have been based on better records, sound regulations, and measures for proper oversight and follow-up. Greece of the 1950s had many children available or "made available" for adoption, but it seldom faced a true emergency—and not even an emergency can excuse inadequate processing or record-keeping. These adoptions happened in the twilight between theory and praxis, between nation (even *omogeneia*) and state, between private and public law, with entrepreneurial individuals taking the lead more often than any state-wide institutions (including the lawcourts, which only rejected petitions for US-bound adoptions in extremely rare cases). Private initiative far outweighed government initiative or policymaking on the Greek side, whereas on the US side, the opposite was true: special immigration provisions conditioned the adoption flows from Greece as well as from other sending countries.

Overseas adoption flows and occasional corrupt adoption practices do elicit shame, conjuring up associations with "third world" countries. Countries eagerly protect their global reputation, and an outpouring of their own children by way of adoption does not make them look good. But shame, silence, or denial have not been the proper responses to the nearly 4,000 lives affected (counting Greek adoptees solely, not even the affected first families). The history of the Cold War Greek adoption movement, however, should not be one of blame or shame but should be about discovery and transparency. In the spirit of transparency and confidentiality, I disclose the real names of only those people who have publicly spoken to or published about the adoption process in which they were involved. Some adoptive parents have mentioned children's names, but I cannot presume that the now adult adoptees would permit me to use their names. For ethical reasons, I protect the intimate details of their lives that some sources might reveal. Also, the playscript has preserved the adoption terminology and the tenor of storytelling used by my interviewees and archival sources, even when some usages may by now appear dated or controversial. Even the Greek word for adoption (υιοθεσία) is itself somewhat of a misnomer, for etymologically identifying the child as male only. "Adoptee" sounds unduly passive. Adopted persons do not like to be reminded how adoption was *done to* them, how their own agency was curtailed, and how they became "adoptlings" or "adopteds." But "adoptee," "birth family," and "adoptive parents" are still terms implicitly sanctioned or effectively advanced by the Greek adoptee community, which is still awaiting its first "insider" participant in the new research field of critical adoption studies. All terms serve a clarificatory, not a value-laden, purpose in this writing. Often, I was the first to interview one of the Greek adoptees, and this practice alone delivered huge validation. This joyful experience was new for me as well, because many of my previous subjects (in Greek theater and politics) had been interviewed many times before and occasionally gave me the rehearsed script. What the adoptees gave me, however, was adoption unrehearsed. Out came the raw truths that are rarely spoken, let alone believed.

I have often caught myself starting conversations with newfound Greek adoptees with the near-apologetic words, "I myself am not an adoptee. I'm writing about things that I have not personally experienced." To commit to a collaborative reading, writing, and staging project then, I needed to answer two questions for myself. The first was, "Can I do this well?" While this question is not for me to answer, my response to myself was, "I think I can do this well if I research this new topic thoroughly enough. I can at least try, in the hope that others who are 'adoption-insiders' will join in." And the second question was, "Is this project confining anyone in the Greek adoptee community who would want to publish their own kind of narrative? Can my project, rather, become a medium that will amplify their voices?" The likely answer to that last question is "yes," given the way publishing works: the more noteworthy one book is, the more likely a publisher will be to take on a similar book in the future. Here again, it helps that *Adoption, Memory, and Cold War Greece* has already answered the important questions of how and how many? How did the adoptions from Greece happen? How many adoptees are we talking about? The book also started the uneasy conversation about how much: how much money was involved? As I give talks about my ongoing research, I take the opportunity to recommend other narratives—first-person accounts, nonfiction books—along with outlining the actual history of what happened over time, what powered the Greek postwar and US-bound adoption movement, and what made it dwindle and vanish. So yes, some people might not want to read a narrative or analysis written by someone who is not an adoptee. But for all those still interested in the many shades of these adoptions and their many unspoken and unspeakable dimensions, please bear with me and focus on the playscript, which does justice to the personal testimonies. Roughly one-third of this edition lets the adoptees speak.

Adoption: The Inside Story, the Story Inside

Adoption, I was to learn although not immediately, is hard to get right.
                                                —Joan Didion, *Blue Nights* (2011: 60)

Adoption, Memory, and Cold War Greece uncovered the history and politics but also the social taboos that undergirded the mass adoptions of young children from destitute 1950s Greece and beyond. The 1950s was still a decade of shattered support networks and overburdened families. The country's faltering infrastructure was slowly being rebuilt, but the lingering ghosts of the Civil War occasionally reemerged. My book stated a cultural as well as a historical critique and a first call to action. It deconstructed one of the most tenacious cultural representations sustaining the interest in international adoption to this day: the myth of humanitarian "rescue." Since the late 1940s, this resilient and self-serving myth has shown its capacity to mute a part of the Greek and Cold War past that merits further scholarly and public attention. The first wave of the Greek-to-American adoption movement was conditioned by postwar geopolitical strategies. It fueled and was fueled by a humanitarianism of a neocolonial make, complete with an undying rhetoric: "poor Greek war orphans" were "saved" by the "benevolent" but rich and powerful Cold War patron. In the thick of the postwar baby boom and the turn from family reconstitution to family creation, the United States soon responded to childless couples' calls for infants with yet more Greek and other foreign adoptees. The stated (but unexamined) wish of couples who "just wanted to have a family" was met with tremendous sympathy, but it wrapped the common perception of "the best interest of the child" in ambiguity, clouding whose best interests were being addressed first. Meanwhile, Greece's Cold War reconstruction economy, that is, its prolonged dependency on American aid and "goodwill," lay at the root of the Greek overseas adoption practice, which became an easy proxy or substitute for building a domestic welfare system.

The Western-oriented humanitarian ideal of "saving" children, preferably white "orphans," made that in-country adoptions or other solutions were not properly considered. Stavroula Pipyrou has introduced the concepts of "armed love" and of the "violence of humanitarianism," demonstrating the inconsiderate to cruel effects of oft-expedient humanitarianism that serves political agendas (2020). In this light, many Greek adoptions may be characterized as drastic or violent humanitarian interventions premised on the care for children. International adoptions, or adoptions of no return, based on poor preparations, hasty procedures, and lack of monitoring, became casualties of the unintentional consequences of care. Since the late 1940s, overseas adoptions have remained enmeshed in policymaking strategies and foreign relations, sometimes in foreign military operations, which explains why aid policy and practice can diverge so widely. Pipyrou refers to the same time period of the early 1950s but to internal acts of "saving" children, in her detailed analysis of traumatic child displacements from flood-stricken areas of Calabria, South Italy. She also describes the fog of silence that has long enveloped these "casualties of care." She credits the terms to Miriam Ticktin (2011) whose research on unfair immigration policies and practices in France has culminated in her book *Casualties of Care*.[6] One may add Gordon Lynch's *Wounds of Charity*, emphasizing the risks as well as the promises of humanitarian involvement.[7] Pipyrou elaborates on the theme of silence, the silence of the state but also the child victims' silencing of their PTSD-like state. The theme of the otherwise very expressive nature of silence, of un-voicing, is a topic that permeates our playscript, which pays attention to childhood trauma and re-traumatization.[8]

This edition positions itself at the opposite end of adopt-splaining by anyone but the adoptee. The playscript un-silences (the histories of) the 4,000 Greek adoptees who were sent to the United States between 1948 and 1975. It draws attention to the microdynamics of adoption, and it provides entry points into the sense of loss and dispossession that the foreign adoption entailed. The status and the questions of those who suffer in silence require recognition and validation. Set against the onset of the global Cold War and the creation and rapid development of international adoption, this playscript is the first one to give voice and body to the biopolitics of the Greek adoption phenomenon.[9] The Greek model of politicized population management through adoption provided the blueprint to subsequent cross-border adoption flows, whose long-term consequences, psychological as well as communal, have only recently become the object of study. I critically invoke life-writing as a way of understanding lives in which adoption from Greece has figured prominently and also the modes in which these lives have been represented. By un-layering the muted mass adoption history of postwar Greece, the playscript delves into new archives, new languages, new time periods, new informant pools, new genres of writing, and new creative and artistic expressions, all of them placing pressure on the master narrative of Greece's 1950s "reconstruction." I challenge historical assumptions about the postwar and Cold War reconstruction, which is heavily tested by the sociopolitical realities of US-Greek relations on the ground in Greece, in the Greek family. Combining history (archival and oral) and creative nonfiction writing, the playscript offers the reader ways to comprehend life histories shaped by adoption from Greece and stories subjugated by Cold War tactics.

Greece's case of mass US-bound adoptions must also claim back the public space and discourse that the binary narratives of the Civil War child evacuation campaigns (*paidomazoma* and *paidofylagma*) have usurped in Greek history-writing covering the postwar years.[10] Other countries, too, have been grappling with their twentieth-century international adoption histories, but Greece has postponed public and critical engagement for the longest span of time—for no less than seventy-five years. The delay of this critique is striking given that Greece was the first state to participate in the intercountry adoption movement, as the international adoption phenomenon was called in its nascent, immediate postwar stage. More than one thousand children had left Greece for the United States by the late summer of 1952, which means, *before* the practice of mass intercountry adoption had even begun to take hold in Korea. The case of Greece functions as a necessary corrective to an oversimplified Cold War and/or anticommunist adoption history, steeped in American "altruism" and reactionary Greek national pride. Greece's case may even claim back some of the public and academic space that one-sided adoption narratives have lent to the massive Korean adoption movement and to the Asian adoption landscape, for pointing out the pitfalls of inaccuracies and faulty chronologies. Therefore, there is no turning away from the long-absent missing link, the Greek US-bound adoption history, for all it can contribute to the burgeoning field of transnational adoption studies. For one, the early 1950s and subsequent mass adoptions from Greece were not impervious to racism. Rather, they add nuance to the dimensions of race, given that racism was different but far from absent in the Greek cases. Only from the mid-1950s on did US-bound adoptions from Korea made overseas adoption more visible and more racially charged. There is no turning away, either, from the Greek adoptees' personal stories, which, perhaps for lack of earlier and serious recognition, the aging adoptees themselves are now eager to share. Our playscript participates in, but also reassesses, a larger trend to "decolonize" international adoption, which has opened rapidly to narratives of displacement, disruption, and loss. The Greek adoptees' seemingly *local* identity, as Greek-to-American or Greek-to-Dutch adoptees, is one of *global* identification when studied under the current lens of displacement and migration. Together, the Greek adoptees produce a highly contemporary narrative of displacement that refracts in many shades but that also, again collectively, constitutes the narrative that displaces. Beyond the initial shock to the Greek historical master narrative, this mass adoption history lends itself exceedingly well to public debate and civic engagement, which need to take place now and in the immediate future. It is to the subterranean adoptee narrative that I want to give critical and public voice—the adoptees' voices and that of my own—the voice that links current displacement to mid-twentieth-century conditions and invites an exchange of ideas among our readers (and spectators).

The goal of the playscript as an adoptee-centric, collective, and critical writing project is to advance knowledge in international adoption studies but also to provide deeper qualitative insight and greater authenticity. Through the voices, including the unsettling voices, of many different stakeholders in the Greek adoption phenomenon, the playscript produces a slab of social history constructed from "below," building on unusual cornerstones such as witness testimonies, legal maneuverings, "market" data, detective work, and investigative journalism. The fine-grained, intimate form of the social history underpinning the playscript compels us to revisit Cold War Europe and to rethink its histories of displacement and their repercussions on ordinary lives. The conceptual approach of critical life-writing undergirds my own choice, not of a topic, but of an issue, the big issue that is innocent people's lives. Our play is, therefore, as much about reading, recording, and collecting as it is about listening and advocating—reckoning with adoption. It grapples with the fraught business of adopting, being adopted, and not being adopted enough. It captures, for the first time, the entangled, prolonged, even protracted narrative that is adoption from Greece, or adoption at large. Therefore, the life stories, testimonies, and records collected and analyzed here must speak to the rare, psychological documentation of a different time and place, and of the journeying in between. The stories' profound emotionality also speaks to a collective analysis of recent Greek history and its efforts to un-silence political and social traumas. My empathetic scholarship may help to unlock the latter realms, especially, to bring history to life but also to show how closely interwoven history is with ordinary life and living human beings. In the ideal life-writing intervention, the academic, the author/editor would not exist, or at least circumscribe her cuts and editorial decisions so as not to alter the story, the experience, the self-analysis. I do not see myself as an author or editor, but rather as a curator, who aids in the presentation of records as objects as well as subjects and thus engages with materialities as well as fluidities. In the literal and Latin sense of the word "curator," I aim to bring *care* to the adoptee lives and stories and, by lending long overdue recognition, a modicum of *cure* as well. I have been very concerned about crossing the line between alliance and appropriation in writing about adoption. Nonetheless, my sympathetic approach may occasionally blur the lines between researcher and subject, given how much it values the adoptees' comradeship in their pursuit of self-realization.

Scope and Methods: Life-Writing

Being a very considerate person she [your birth mother] had full awareness of her poorness and helplessness to bring you up and offered you a good life. Exactly because she wanted for you to have the best kind of care, which would assure you a bright future, and out of love for you she gave her consent to your adoption.

(Response in English written by a Greek social worker and expert in "counseling and root-seeking," addressing a Greek adoptee's request for information, October 21, 2020)

It is the voices of the adoptees that interest me—not the repeated clichés.[11] The play *FTRWM* is not merely a follow-up project; it is a critical and creative life-writing project that was developed for and with Greek adoptees. It sets out to un/recover a powerful, hidden history from the personal and private experiences of individuals. It ponders some of the many ways in which people have understood and produced adoption. How did the post-WWII world think about adoption? How do people think about these same adoptions more than half a century later? What kind of wording did the practitioners involved develop? What kind of wording do the practitioners continue to repeat, even in October 2020, as in the epigraph quoted above? Mothers give up their children out of love? Would that not mean that every person who declares his or her love might well one day walk away? And if the love for a child intersects with possible relinquishment, what kind of a burden does that place on subsequent attachments? How, then, has this enduring but utterly trite language and how have these practices been received by the adoptees themselves?[12] What have been the material signs that expressed imaginings of adoption? How have the adoptees made sense of their adoption if it was "necessary"—and if it could easily have been avoided? Some of the documents introduced in the playscript deliver institutional versions of events; some act as plain data-stories; some push adoption records and personal dealings to their communicative limits. Some I have selected for their legal perspective; some have been emotionally reframed. Entire lives and heaps of memories and emotions are, after all, caught between the lines of official documents, lost to the adoptee ever since those records were first filed away (Figure 1).

FIGURE 1 The author delving into old hospital records in Patras (April 25, 2019). Photograph by the late Ronit Kertsner.

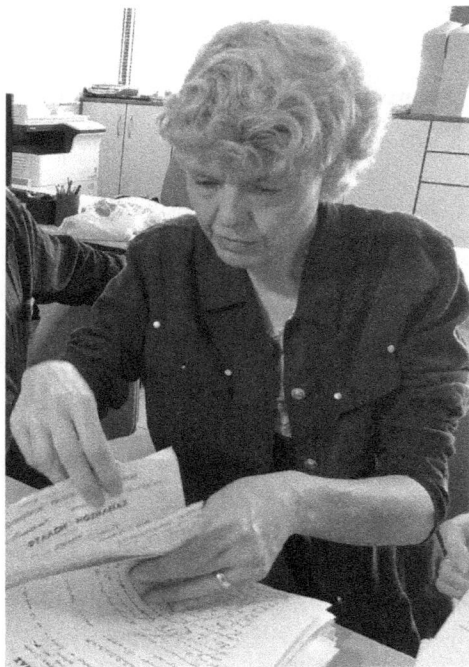

Taking its cue from *Adoption, Memory, and Cold War Greece*, the play *FTRWM* rehistoricizes the Cold War Greek adoption movement, now zooming in on its advantages and setbacks. My 2019 adoption book made the Greek adoption history visible across national borders and languages, but it also acknowledged the many silent stories of abandonment and dys-placement, of adoption disruption and dissolution. *FTRWM*, then, is not just a companion piece to my previous book. It draws more boldly on creative writing and psychology, with references to mid-twentieth-century history and society, to bring personal accounts and testimonies to the forefront. This testimony theater reaches beyond the tools and methods of the social sciences to reconnect with the humanities as well. New insights from the study of child diasporas may meet those gleaned from research in the public humanities and the medical humanities. Inconvenient but documented and stated truths may thus penetrate the realm of activism and policymaking.

Testimony theater was popular in Greece under the military dictatorship of 1967–1974, and it has seen waves of popularity in Central and South America under similar oppressive regimes. The reasons are obvious: directors and playwrights, who present themselves as compilers of multivocal sources, can deliver scripts for the stage that subvert censorship by invoking the authenticity and the third-person authorship of the texts. If these texts bear additional "prestige," for being issued by officials, lawcourts, public intellectuals, or standard history books, then authoritarian regimes have an even harder time trying to muzzle dissenting voices. The director and the playwright typically do not object to seeing their roles reduced; rather, for sourcing the texts and preparing them for the stage, they may present themselves as "tools" of a preexisting critical mindset or discourse—and seek safety in that capacity. But they still play formative and creative roles for deciding on the multimodal selection, the cast, the setting, movement, irony, and tone, in consultation with actors who are courageous enough to step up. Thus, testimony theater may readily become activist theater when it features engaged amateur actors who have experienced the situations they perform, rendering their case even more compelling.[13]

But how does a testimony, oral or written, rise to the level of story? What's in words? I was struck by the simple language of a 2024 obituary: "Mike was born as [...] in Edessa, Greece [...] By the time he was 8 years old, he and his siblings [names] had been adopted by [adoptive parents' names] of Grandview, Mo." What put these adoptions in motion? What family tragedy might lie behind them? Starting deceptively small, I reinvest in the close reading of words, of the varied, multivocal texts produced by the adoptees themselves and also by other members of the "adoption triad" (the birth parents and adoptive parents in addition to the adoptee). We prefer, rather, the term adoption "constellation," given that the word "triad" implies that all sides of the "adoption triangle" would be equal and would have received equitable treatment, which has historically not been the case.[14] Scholarship has not yet seen the nuances to the predicament of *all* parties and, most significantly, it has missed the legacy of pain across continents and generations.

FTRWM features various forms or genres of life-writing that are all modes of writing, or otherwise capturing, Greek adoptee life, and they include the materiality of official documents, images, and objects as well. My aim has been to find these forms, foreground them, solicit interpretations of them, and analyze them, not only for their "truth" value, but also as modes of expression that speak searchingly to the embellished picture of the adoption flow from "poor" Greece to "prosperous" and "generous" America. Adoptee stories and memoirs "de-essentialize" the genre of life-writing in terms of its older and ethically imposed "connection to the 'truth,'" maintains Jenny Heijun Wills.[15] Not infrequently, adoption documents do not tell the whole truth. Adoption explanations tend to present the kind of adoption that never quite was. The truth of the adoptee is authentic, but the process of mining memory, fact-finding, and fact-revising is always ongoing, which leaves "truth" open to redefinition, as a truth to the best of one's abilities, to the best of one's knowledge at any given moment in a lifelong quest. An identity based on unconnected dots or preliminary truths, therefore, feels like a provisional identity, like an identity to be completed by way of an "identity reveal." Greek adoptee Mary Cardaras writes, in an unpublished essay titled "Identity":

> Details seem to have changed. Some details that I thought were true, are not. Others have emerged that are entirely new to me. There is no way to hold onto anything for certain, to be able to say with any degree of confidence, this I know to be absolutely true. What is certain is the uncertain, the irretrievable, the non-confirmable. Except only these two, indisputable facts: Adopted. Born Greek.[16]

Thus, as a gamut of post-positivist forms and methods, life-writing offers advantages and vantage points that other genres of writing or analytical treatments might foreclose. Mark Mazower (2017) has placed his family's experience at the center of a wide-ranging historical analysis of twentieth-century European history. Joanna Eleftheriou (2020), author of the memoir *This Way Back*, defends Annette Kuhn's position that individual experience should have a place in critical writing.[17] My own voice sounds through in direct speech on only a few occasions in the play; otherwise, the voices of the adoptees prevail. Cardaras goes on to touch on many important issues, which are also at the core of the play:

> Throughout my life, I was reminded of my otherness. My difference. I was always the baby adopted from Greece. I was the baby on the boat, the one who was passed around to the other passengers so they could play with me, hold me, soothe me as we crossed the Atlantic to America. Often people ask about my "real" parents and where I "really" come from and to whom I "really" belong. They also never fail to include an addendum, a closing comment about me vis-à-vis my origins. Like this: "This is Mary's brother. They were adopted ..." Or "These are Mary's parents, but she was adopted ..." Or "Mary looks like her mother, *but* she was adopted." Furthermore, others have negated my feelings, without malice nor any awareness of what they were saying about the reality of my experience, by minimizing my adoption itself. "You were too young to remember anything" or "you're not really an immigrant. You were a baby." Those folks entirely miss the essence of my existence.

My aim, our aim, has been to contribute to transnational discussions in adoption studies with a research-and-reality project that must convey new content and prefigure new form. When the adoptees' scant documents see the light of day, sometimes through unrelenting searches but often, too, through sheer accidents of serendipity, they make other "data" disappear, dispelling myths and burnished stories. Adoptee quests push the limits on the searcher's willingness to let the unexpected happen, and to overcome disappointment when answers that one can reasonably expect are far from forthcoming. The approach of embracing the unusual and the serendipitous does not sound methodological at all, and yet it is better viewed as another open-ended strategy, appropriate to this subject. In interviews with adoptees, I listened carefully and only asked occasional questions. I told them that they should tell me only what they were entirely comfortable sharing with me—and that would be all I wanted to hear. When I wrote down the testimonies afterward, I tried to preserve the informants' particular way of speaking and the warmth or the chill of their voices. When adoptees submitted their own texts, I only corrected some typographical errors and implemented a few minor edits for consistency. I asked adoptees to write about their own experiences, to become the authors of their own lives. I encouraged people to write the first-draft story that worked for them, after decades of taking their lives to the ever-next phase of potential and strength. Not all personal stories have a clear beginning, even if they have a middle and an end. Some narrations may never gain a beginning even as more data and new interpretations come in.

So many people have asked me how I have been finding the Greek adoptees. At the start of this project in 2013, I had to look for Greek adoptee-informants. To cover the early phase, I credit personal connections, the contacts of contacts, the occasions of public lectures—and again some mind-boggling serendipities. Now, however, and through networking on social media platforms, the Greek adoptees are stepping out in public and are spontaneously identifying themselves.

FTRWM presents the Greek adoption narrative by way of both individual and collective stories. Together we reclaim the adoptee narrative, one story at a time. Also, these narrations are not meant to make for riveting reading. Rather, they are about searing memories into writing, so they cannot be forgotten. Some adoptees mentioned a teenage journal, whether affectionately or dismissively, and I asked them to dig it up. The force of their childhood or youthful literality re-created family and institutionalized spaces—areas of intensities that were not self-evident. We devised various ways in which the first-hand experience of adoption could be transformed into text and testimony, visual image, and message. I value the double movement of complicity and critique enacted by the collective playscript that we built up from raw material for theatrical expression. Significantly, this kind of public exchange and dissemination posits adoptees as owners of their emotions and experts on their experiences—again a long overdue recognition. Together, we continue to create unexpected ties between subject and researcher—and occasionally reverse the roles.

The adoptees' life-writing has been about crafting a narrative that links together events, experiences, and perceptions, with opportunities to add relief to an inevitably hybrid identity. Some adoptees hesitated to include in their texts any details about their adoptive parents, for fear of appearing ungrateful, even though they realized that such details make the stories more real and believable. For those who barely survived a bad adoption, the writing process took great effort, often stymied by the fear of upsetting the adults, of disappointing the third parties (including me). Yet they agreed that it remains important to write about the wordless wounds, rather than letting non-adopted persons tell about their experiences. Some adoptees spoke to not just surviving but transcending bad situations, whose aftereffects they are still trying to navigate. Rather than distinguishing between "good" and "bad" adoptions, however, we now believe that adoptions map onto an imaginary (but no less "real") spectrum of emotions, which may well be at variance with the antithetical extremes. Thus, the effort-topic of collective writing underwent its own becoming, beyond the superficial spread of wording. Notably, the adoptees' written and also spoken experiences counter the general public's stubborn determination to read an adoption narrative as a story of triumph or redemption, as a win–win situation. Collective life-writing proves to be a good tool with which to redress the typical spinning of adoption into a fairytale. When the adoptees speak for and among themselves, they dare to bring the unresolved to their/the story. They express a burden for being tasked by the what-if, while some known answers tether them to the past. Together with the Greek adoptees, the play ponders the "have-beens" but also the "might-have-beens," elusive as they may be.

Together, we have watched the fog of silence of some seventy-five years dissipate. We have observed people breaking out of their isolation, to see their experience validated. In a first phase, the adoptees derived empowerment from the realization that somebody was finally proving that this Greek adoption history even happened. In subsequent phases, the adoptees have felt empowered to share their writings, to blog or publish in print, to speak out on Greek citizenship or American deportation. But for the Greek adoptee community's story to become integrated in the grand narrative of Greece's history is still a distant goal. It is this last phase, of the adoptees speaking and advocating for themselves, that is the most important one. It is also the only one that can help dispel negative stereotypes about "ill-adjusted" or "ungrateful" adoptees. All too often, adoptees are spoken *for* and decided *for*, and thus held captive in a "state of perpetual childhood."[18] Once adopted means always adopted, without a "before" or "after." Life-writing expands significantly when adoptees move from issues of identity negotiation to more activist critiques of the practices of their own and subsequent international adoptions. This gradual transformation then presses the question: What is the cultural-political significance of the adoptee testimonies today? Can these testimonies become vehicles for adoption reform? How can they inform contemporary debates about international adoption in the Western world?

For the Life of Me: A Revisionist Adoption History

I come from crossing oceans
to find myself. I come from deep issues
and shallow solutions.
[...]
I come from unanswered
questions and unread books, unnoticed
effort and undelivered apologies
[...]
I come from looking in the mirror
and looking online to find myself.

—Dean Atta, *The Black Flamingo* (2019, 217–218)

The stories and insights in *FTRWM* speak to everyone's struggle to be included, in a family, in a society, in a country, in a religion, in a language group, in a birth register, in civic and legal structures. They are about be-longing, too, being all about longing. The play makes Greece once more central to the post-WWII international adoption movement, but this time, the (hi)stories and experiences, intertwined with the universal themes of identity, belonging, and loss touch everyone, whether one has been affected by adoption or not. About fifty percent of the general population is either directly or indirectly affected by adoption and nearly all of us care for identifying practices. Every extended Greek family seems to have been close to the phenomenon of either international or in-country adoption, sometimes to both. But silence on the topic still haunts many Greek families. My 2019 book and *FTRWM* unmask the mechanisms of the unilateral and often forced migration that spurred the adoptions of young children from postwar Greece and that took a tremendous personal toll: the "undesirables" of a muted past have paid a heavy and lifelong price for the adoptions over which they themselves did not have any control, and the mothers and families who gave up children faced a lifetime of loss and brokenness. Therefore, our work demonstrates that international adoption of the Cold War era, far from being a personal or a peripheral matter, was central to the experience and constitution of the American as well as the Greek sociopolitical realms and that it entailed the hurt caused by the many degrees of "forced adoptions," based on questionable practices. In the new field of the revisionist history of child adoption that must lead to policy reform, the play issues a call to action, to ask, more urgently than ever, that the Greek state and the main government and private archives open their records to the Greek-born adoptees of the 1950s through 1960s, whose birth families may still be found. It is our hope that, after years of loss and losing, of suffering and searching, there would finally be someone or something to be found. Adoption of an infant is, after all, a form of family disruption before it is family formation; there is deep loss before there is even the possibility of gain. This sense of loss anchors the play, but it can be somewhat healed by the joy of finding, given how transformational the journey of searching and reuniting—and of finding the words—can be. At times, however, Greece is just a foreign land, throwing up difficult borders, especially that of its forbidding language, leaving the adoptee with the feeling of being uprooted, rerooted, rerouted.

Because the subject of the foreign adoptions has long contained and limited the past, it has left many issues of the present unresolved. Adoptees born in Greece of the 1940s through early 1960s, like many others from different but again dependent sending countries, live with the unresolved questions and consequences of the past. Given this backdrop and burden, my 2019 book has stirred up some controversy but has overall been well received. Many Greek adoptees have embraced my book for what it dares to state; many, too, have felt that it should have been theirs to state. I could not agree more. For decades now, the adoptees have been surrounded by others ready to comment on their adoptions on their behalf, whether they were the adoptive parents, the agencies or middlemen, or just random strangers, who called them "very lucky" and characterized them as "so totally American by now." Adoptees have long resented the colonial undertones that keep referring to the "lucky" "orphan" that was given access to "far superior" families, institutions, papers, politics, lifestyles—while their first parents were not assisted or were obstructed in their own right and desire to parent. After all, imperialist and neocolonial myths talked of "rescue missions" and promised the adoptees' smooth assimilation, but hardly anyone ever checked with the "blank slate" children whether they were doing well and kept doing well. Surely, adoptee resentment is not appreciated, not ever. "Becoming a blank slate on arrival was the considerate thing to do," rejoins a foreign adoptee from South Korea, who gives voice to the sentiments of many more cross-border adoptees. She continues, "Like so many things that were out of my control and chosen for me, I felt like even my own my emotions were not mine to feel—or at least to express."[19] Besides, adoptees arrived in homes where the adoptive parents were far from clean slates themselves. The adopters thought of the child as ready for fresh imprints, but they did not think of themselves in the same way. Therefore, the time has come to create new meaning on the topic of international adoption, and to allow this meaning to come forward, to find its audience through a bolder and more interactive form of writing. The faces and fates of the actual adoptees must emerge from behind the analyses and the numbers, which should not vacate personal-historical particularities. Consistent with the 2019 published history, I focus once more on Greece as a case study with wider dimensions, a case study that appeals to all those exploring their own voices in new contents and formats. Critical life-writing is our preferred lens, offering greater versatility in voices, emotions, genres, and sources, while accommodating any levels of the incompleteness or the constructedness of the writing. We aim to deliver innovative forms of life-writing, in which formal and personal archive meet one another and intersect with genealogical and affective readings as well as with ideological subject positions.

My Greek adoption history was based on a carefully compiled archive of hard evidence. Here it may serve as a referential framework for developing more complex historical and cultural sensibilities. My earlier writing, as well as my style of documenting, incorporated succinct forms of witness testimonies and the first samples of broader cultural representations of the Greek adoptions.

With that background firmly in place, the play *FTRWM* can now delve into the—unorganized—archive of the emotions and bring the people involved into clearer focus (while protecting their anonymity, if they so wish). I am eager to give faces and voices to those affected, and to do so in a style of writing that analytic approaches might otherwise undercut. This new project pursues a different type of scientific knowledge: it seeks insights that emerge from and with the Greek adoptees and, again, enrich the history of adoption (beyond what the behavioral sciences have to offer). It strives to realize the potential of life-writing in the development of twenty-first-century disciplines of study, such as the recent adoption histories. Since its emergence two decades ago, the subfield of the history(ies) of international adoption flows has tried hard to step out of national frameworks, and it has championed transnational, transcultural, and multidirectional approaches to intercountry adoption. It has also welcomed collections of adoption stories, some still organized along geographical lines. My involvement with the Greek adoptee experiences may seem to bring back a nationally oriented approach, but my concern with the adoptees' American (or other) living experiences widens the horizon. The seemingly personal history of the foreign-born adoptees is also the history of some of the volatile but defining aspects of mid-twentieth-century America. It discloses the ways in which foreign adoption has inscribed itself in the collective memory of the Cold War, in small as well as in large urban communities. While adoption itself may be at the heart of personal and local histories, the issue of foreign adoption, in all its varieties, is by no means limited to the familial or local sphere but extends to national and global planes. Now that the issue has garnered international scholarly attention, it calls for a continuing exchange of insights and conclusions, which the voices of the participants in adoption cannot but revise and strengthen.

Moreover, I debunk the homogeneity of the (similarly formatted and presented) collections of adoption stories, doing justice to a realm in which no two adoptions or adoption stories are ever the same, not even within the same adoptive family. The versatility of the life-writing formats invoked here bespeaks the wide variety that characterizes the phenomenon of adoption itself. The vehicle of life-writing, steeped in concerns with identity-seeking and self-realization, becomes an apt medium to properly convey the sentiments and the sensibilities of the intricate adoptee networks. Therefore, too, I have not made any changes to the literal truth of the diverse texts presented in the play. From a conceptual/theoretical angle, *FTRWM* taps into currents that draw on autobiographical and memoir writing, but it reaches beyond them to advance life-writing and its openness to alternative formats and to the toolmarks of the composition process. Adoption stories, even in their thumbnail forms, carry a lot of narrative capital, especially when they dwell on the vicissitudes of relatedness, which, for being about family relations, have a very specific and yet universal quality to them. Life-writing lays bare those narrative strategies that foreground human relations, intimate relations. Social life is, after all, about the art of constructing and maintaining relationships. The formats I have chosen to cover in *FTRWM*, however, take life-writing forward for being less traditional formats, much more succinct, and also more poignant. They are the texts, too, of people who are not trained writers. These factors prompt my critical reflection, once more, on the adoptee's life-writing as a process, not just as a product. Also, I restore to the adoptees the kind of agency that derives from choosing, writing, and polishing—from taking charge of their own stories.

FTRWM prioritizes the Greek adoptee voices and experiences. It values the stories as lynchpins that connect adoption and culture in its broadest sense. It aims to advance debates across disciplines, not only on family studies and the construction of childhood, but also on the potential of "authoring" adoption as a lifelong process. Life-writing formats enable us to reflect on the precarious modalities of adoption in terms of questions, hypotheses, speculations about a possible other life. The playscript speaks to the intersections of creative life-writing and transnational studies, of the geography and sociology of adoption and kinship, which are vested also in the (un)knowability of the human subject. It ties in with Cold War history that interfaces with other areas such as global culture and society, art and identity. The important questions raised by *FTRWM* probe well beyond descent, ethnic composition, or geostrategic location. Other displaced groups of people, too, will find resources in the very personal life-writing contributions collected here, which speak to universally recognizable experiences. These experiences answer to the questions of who are among the most vulnerable in a society and how do we treat them—and what does our treatment indicate about the strength of the democratic justice we proclaim? Even though the vast majority of the Greek children were adopted by the most normative of American and Dutch couples (white, middle-class, heterosexual, and married), their voices challenge and subvert ethnically inward-looking master narratives, in a country, Greece, where ethnic myths link to national myths of classical Greek ancestry, and also in a superpower, the United States, where "patriotic" myths are being revamped on a near-daily basis. For the Greek adoptee, genetic origin is one and certain (with DNA tests results to prove it), and yet his/her personal history of the past sixty to seventy-five years is "other." The adoptees' writing is, therefore, enriched by further layers of complexity, amid the pull of two very strong nationalist, essentialist, and occasionally chauvinist forces, none of them able to deliver satisfactory "wholeness." The now more vocal presence of the hundreds of Greek adoptees who were abandoned children must counter any prescribed nationalist narrative (Greece), while it also challenges the redemptive narrative of reconstruction, democratization, and hard-earned humanitarianism (USA).

Raw Writing

I come from my own pen but I see
people torn apart like paper, each a story
or poem that never made it into a book.
—Dean Atta, *The Black Flamingo* (2019, 218)

FTRWM espouses an innovative as well as a critical approach, in which creativity meets criticism. It blends adoptee testimonies and private musings, the unfiltered verbatim and the contemplative, the cautious and the crazy, into a dialogue, open and expansive. Also, the script downplays the authoritative voice of the observer, or the analysis of the historian, to encompass, rather, verbal, visual, and also virtual modes of adoptee expression. It integrates other people's voices, images, poems, documents, case histories, journal entries, email communications, Facebook postings, even rants. After years of polishing my writing to no end, I now venture out on a different track: that of raw writing instead of constant rewriting. I strongly feel that, as "raw material" in the act of raw writing, the material does greater justice to the adoptees' still raw emotions, about which, it turns out, female adoptees are more ready to speak or write. While I resist the tendency to re-feminize the world of adoption and child-rearing, I have no satisfactory explanation for this phenomenon, other than to state that female adoptees also lead in the underexplored domains of adoption-related online networking, searching, documenting, and publishing. My impressions are merely empirically informed, but they are corroborated by the similar conclusions of the astute observers of other, younger adoptee networks, activist groups, and research circles. In terms of raw writing, this reflection implies that empirical knowledge, too, remains a rawly hewn building block of a psychosocial and intellectual edifice that is still very much under construction.

Without being overtaken or overwritten by the authorial voice, *FTRWM* presents much material in its unadorned and unmediated form, as if it were the unedited historic footage that serves as the ideal starting point to the documentary filmmaker seeking authenticity. The adoptees' writing incorporated here reflects (and inflects) the process of their constructing of identity by way of raw materials, the edgy, nonlinear, and fragmented pieces of their identity. This script's composition, too, integrates raw emotional threads, interweaving pain, frustration, anguish, and the sense of grief and loss caused by foreign adoption. Also, the undiluted writing that the playscript deliberately preserves must remind us of adoptee management as if it were the management of the material resources of the country of origin. It must recall the adoptee pool's state of becoming the nation's raw material for export, against the backdrop of asymmetrical postwar power relations. As adoptable "goods," children were moved to a supposedly superior receiving country or community, but the colonizing—and dehumanizing—nature of this transfer has not yet been properly acknowledged.[20] The crude materiality of these exports is all the more striking as they are discussed in the watered-down terms of (supposedly harmless) fluidity: they come in "flows," "waves," "outpourings." "Are we about to see a worldwide children's market develop, much like a world market in raw materials and labor forces," asked a 1984 Dutch police report with some alarm, but with little sense of how widespread the phenomenon had already become and how big it had yet to grow.[21] Faced with a rapidly globalizing *stork* market, trading in children as commodities, not even trained investigators or experts otherwise realized just how precarious the futures were—the futures of the child adoptees, that is. During the past decade of researching the Greek adoption history, I have come to view the Greek phenomenon through the eyes of people who still live this history every single day. But I have also had misgivings about speaking for the adoptees. So why not let the adoptees and the specific circumstances speak for themselves, raw though they may still be? The verbatim words of the adoptees and of others involved in the adoptions deliver much more accurate personality depictions and affective portraits than I could possibly draw.[22]

Foreign adoption interrogates the family unit, testing the all-too-human need for safety, stability, and belonging—for overcoming any disruptions. It stretches the fabric of the family in its most intimate folds. Very little frank language has ever been spoken about the Greek exports of children that helped build American families by design. *FTRWM* adds frankness to what has, in the Greek and American spheres at least, often been presented as a Hollywood picture, with the guaranteed happy ending that must appease our collective conscience. Adoptees and their sorrow have remained hidden in full view, because adoption had to valorize the nuclear, normative, and "normal" family. Consistent with the pursuit of raw writing, the play comes clean about abandonment, opportunism, retaliation, and sheer cruelty in families that had the option of building something better, but that chose pettiness over generosity of spirit, or money over immaterial rewards. The play's writings by adoption "initiates" burrow under the skin for exposing histories of adversity within the new family. *FTRWM* is ultimately about the fragility as well as the strength of human relationships, of those between parents and children, of individuals to their history and to their evolving selves.

As a forum in print and on stage, *FTRWM* lets Greek adoptees speak for themselves. To this day, many adoption-related topics may be avoided for personal or psychological reasons, and it remains important to protect the privacy of interviewees. Much more remains to be done and can be done, however, with the stories written by the adoptees, including the personal records that they or their own descendants have wanted to share with readers across the globe. By way of their life stories, Greek adoptees are now writing themselves back into Greek history and into Cold War history. The first Greek-to-American adoptee memoirs appeared in self-published formats in 2011. Since then, Greek adoptee stories have appeared in hybrid tones and sizes, and the storytellers themselves have shown varying degrees of literary ambition. The book-length memoirs show how children's existence as adoptees-to-be was repeatedly intercepted by geopolitical events, highlighting the interplay between historical currents and family dynamics. No Greek first parent has, to this day, published the story of losing a child to international adoption. The adoptee memoirs and texts contribute to the project of revisionist history-writing, and first parents' accounts would be very welcome additions. This kind of material is analytically significant if we want to add further nuance to the experiences from memory and postmemory (because the adoptees' identities have infused the lived experiences of their own children). The stories, long or short, prompt us to reconsider the value of testimonies generated on the American side of the Atlantic and to reckon with the impressions and reactions of the postadoptees (if we may so characterize the deferred or mediated experience of adoption by those of the second generation). The desired level of minute personal detail, however, may only be uncovered later, when more classified files and life stories become accessible.

As an academic, one does not easily cross over to the realm of life-writing and memoir or autobiography, especially when that realm in Greece has long been dominated by male politicians of a certain age, who are eager to shape their legacy. Traditionally, this kind of (auto)biographical writing has bled into Greek history-writing and into the making of contemporary public history, which still struggles to break the dynastic mold, the partisan politics and personalities. Contemporary Greece, after all, tends to read politics as real life, removed from political theory. For Greek social history, therefore, to "talk back," for the Greek adoptees to speak for themselves and to do so from abroad is a big and very timely step forward. It is nothing short of an intervention, and hopefully one of ad-vent, one that has arrived and is here to stay.

Through critical life-writing, *FTRWM* shifts historical memory and storytelling further away from established patriarchal modes and engages, together with adoptees, in the long, fraught business of becoming. How does one become someone, or someone else, halfway around the world? How does one heal from the shock of radical uprooting? Can one forget when the lack of answers about what happened and how it happened is ever-present? And what if the absence of paperwork is burdened also by the lingering suspicion of illegality? The recent genealogical turn and the mass public enthusiasm for DNA testing have popularized adoption stories with belated reunions.[23] Adoption quests are exciting puzzles in genealogy for those looking on adoption from the outside in. But uncovering the hidden, silenced, and gendered side of genealogy that adoption represents remains an urgent matter of study, to which raw life-writing can contribute substantially. Surely, learning potentially life-saving information about one's family's health history via DNA testing is a boon, but adoptees have so much more at stake. Also, while the quantitative data pools are growing, more comprehensive and subject-driven interpretations cannot stay behind. The various, versatile sources and testimonies here explore the raw memory of the past and especially the subjective space of the young individual. Through raw life-writing, this project sets up an up-to-date framework for examining the positionality of the Greek-born adoptees from a more subjective angle.

The Greek adoptees have not yet mobilized in ways comparable to the vocal Korean adoption rights activists, but the lack of records and the official "policy" of amnesia have been salient and hurtful for them, too. The various strands of the play's collaborative knowledge-making project are unified by the kind of activist message that must help overcome the common sense of loss: directly and indirectly, our texts raise the importance of the moral responsibility of the Greek government to facilitate the adoptees' quests for their genetic history. First, the Greek state succumbed to political, economic, and social pressures of the Cold War period to adopt out more than three thousand of its children. Second, the Greek state has failed to create a responsible body to investigate the nature and numbers of the foreign adoptions that have taken place since the postwar era. With this unified message, we hope to put an end to long-time practices of exclusion and dismissal. Otherwise, the searching adoptees will be left in the labyrinth of the open-ended quest that, for the Greek administration which only reluctantly recognizes them as Greek citizens, merely confirms the suspended and indefinite state of their being. I hope that the production of knowledge on the Greek case will inspire other adoption histories and life-writing initiatives, in which the adoptees will gain recognition as "experience experts," not for having studied a certain condition but for having lived it. As the subjectivity of the adoptees comes into full view, so will the tensions between official policies and individual priorities. Also, with an array of documentation and voices, in which case stories blend with (auto)biographical components and the visual arts, important social and gender issues emerge that hold currency for the demands for social justice today: abuse in child placement, adoptee deportation, wrongful removal, forced adoptions (based on coerced consent), the improper financial gain of unethical adoption brokers, and so on.

International Adoption: *Who(m)* Did It Cost?

Figure 2 proves that international adoption comes with costs attached. This financial document of the minute micro level illustrates what becomes an expansive postwar economy of American family formation. The adoptive mother of one Greek adoptee kept a list of expenses, meticulously typed up and added up, down to the telephone calls and the postage fees. Did the adoption go down as costing the new family? Did the family take a financial loss? Was Maria, the adopted child, allowed to keep a list, if only a vague mental one, of her losses? Did Maria enter a family in which she was made to feel as if she had

FIGURE 2 The price to pay for the adoptee. List of adoption expenses kept by Maria Heckinger's American mother, 1955–1956. Photograph by Maria Heckinger.

```
                    ADOPTION EXPENSES - MARIA


   1955

          August 20th - ARRC Adm Exp              $100.00
          Sept. 26th - Court Costs                 150.00

   1956

          Trip to San Francisco
             ( Telephone Calls - January            10.12
             ( Telephone Calls - February            1.25
             ( Lawyer - draw papers                  5.00
             ( Postage (mail papers to Greece)       2.00
             ( Pictures (our request)                1.00
             ( Tickets to San Francisco (train)     23.92
             ( Tickets from San Fran. (Plane)       35.07
             ( Drawing Documents-Greek Consulate    28.76
             ( Food - Taxis, etc-San Francisco      20.00
             ── Plane Ticket TWA- Greece to N.Y.    269.00
                   (incl clothing expense)
             Plane Ticket TWA - New York to
                            San Diego               87.40
             Escort from San Diego to
                       Chicago and back            150.00
             Telephone calls                        25.00

          Hospital and Doctor                      245.00
             (This figure includes a
             cut on the head and shots)
          (Announcements)                            8.74
                                                 $1162.26
```

to live up to the financial investment that was made in her? Was the priceless child price-tagged for ever after?[24] Or price-gagged? Korean adoption scholar Kimberly McKee concurs: "Adoptees encounter the weight of the financial expenses in combination with the incalculable load of savior narratives."[25] Who(m) did the intercountry adoption really cost? And for how long? Is Maria free enough to tell today? Or is she in debt "for a lifetime"?

The study of Greek migration to the United States may have left us with a general picture of more than two centuries of "modern" migration. But, by the same token, this general view has focused on men or on adults at best, not on children.[26] Even a study of Greek families settling abroad may overlook complexities of kinning and child placement at the ground level. Traditional studies have not afforded a close-up, detailed view of this postwar, US-bound Greek adoption movement, which was merely absorbed into larger, adult migratory trends. Against this backdrop, this edition is innovative, too, for exploring the ways and modes in which children of an involuntary diaspora relate to their homeland. Scholars have yet to explore the impact of diasporic trends and transnationalism on childhood, but Cold War intercountry adoption provides us with a unique vantage point to engage in this exploration and to do so via life-writing. Cold War dynamics made the US present itself as a global leader of international humanitarianism. Dependent Greece started routing children abroad for adoption, to circumscribe cases of unwed motherhood and as a substitute for creating adequate childcare infrastructure. Adoption overseas as a type of welfare intervention… Well through the 1950s, however, this dynamic would have been interpreted as "poor" Greece eagerly accepting foreign "aid."

Accessing forgotten strata of the Greek American diasporic or migratory history, my life-writing project on the US-bound exports of Greek children informs my broader critique of the human cost of dependencies on the Western capitalist model. A study of the overseas adoption traffic from Cold War Greece by way of the adoptee voices and family narratives prompts me to think about this migration flow in the very current terms of dislocation, the separation of children from their parents, and the threat of traumatic family disruption. Unaccompanied and unprotected minors keep moving toward an ambiguous, ever-contingent "American" identity, which risks being dismissed by the hardening rhetoric of American "homeland security." This project makes me reassess also how boundary shifts between public and private initiatives occur and how individual lives may be subjected to the extremes of prolonged secrecy and extravagant publicity, often near-simultaneously but at opposite ends of the world. In the United States as the prime receiving country of the Cold War period, the adoption experience has only gradually been reshaped into a more diversified history and personalized story, in which the subjective and the cultural overshadow the political, which has prevailed in Greece. But a major concern has remained and is at the play's core: *How* to tell the detailed history and individual stories of the Greek adoption phenomenon, allowing, as per the adoptees' wishes, the modern, creative forms to be as important as the contents; *how* to do justice to critical and from-the-heart stories that have never been told before? The originality of *FTRWM* stems from its concerted effort to reconceptualize its subject and subjects across different media within the cultural as well as the private sphere. Here, the personal and the cultural texts, and the artifacts of cultural representations of any kind, are not viewed in isolation but are embedded in a web of interrelations, not unlike the Cold War adoption networks themselves—not unlike seemingly lasting relations of inequity. Thus, the play unmasks the elusive final destination of adoption itself.

NOTES

1 The title *For Three Refrigerators and a Washing Machine* alludes to the fact that the Babies' Center Mitera accepted a donation of three refrigerators and one washing machine from the Netherlands. The Babies' Center then agreed to the adoption of 600 Greek children by Dutch parents over the course of some fifteen years (approximately 1960–1975). With Kyriaki Mitsou, the director of the October 2024 premiere production of the play, we decided not to disclose the meaning of the title until the related scene of the performance revealed it.

2 Since 2008, the United Nations Refugee Agency (UNHCR, 2008) has updated its definition of the "best interests of the child" (note the plural), in a volume of 2021, available online: https://www.refworld.org/pdfid/5c18d7254.pdf. Adoption, however, is hardly discussed and is promptly relegated to the national authorities and domestic jurisprudence (2021, 35, 139).

3 Psychologist Nancy Newton Verrier has long described the range of emotions experienced by the adoptee and the other members of the "adoption triad." Her oft-reprinted book *The Primal Wound* focuses on the effects on relinquished children of separation from the birth mother. See especially Verrier (2012, 20–21, 177–179) and also Glaser (2021, 274). Despite occasional criticism, the book has withstood the test of time, and many adoptees invoke it frequently. Recently, psychotherapists and trauma experts have more vocally recognized the preverbal trauma that the adoptee suffers at the moment of separation from the birth mother, namely the loss of all that was once familiar and comforting, which the infant perceives as a life-threatening shock. Of such a horrendous shock, "the body keeps the score," to use Bessel van der Kolk's (2014) characterization of trauma, post-traumatic stress, and their multiple effects. See also Jules Alvarado's (2020) statement, which is based on her long career in the field, and Grace Newton (2022), who writes from the perspective of the Chinese adoptee and scholar. Newton introduces the productive concept of "trauma of consciousness," which she defines as "the trauma of simply knowing that

violent, oppressive, and exploitative acts have happened in history and are currently happening to people with whom one shares an identity" (2022, 4). For the most recent acknowledgment of adoption trauma, see the contributions to the volume edited by Bertocci, Deeg, and Mayers (2024).

4 Van Steen (2021).

5 Van Steen (2019, 44, 57–61).

6 Pipyrou (2020, 438).

7 The title of Lynch's 2016 book refers to the child migrations from the UK to Canada and Australia, which were handled by religious charities or institutions. See also Lynch (2020).

8 Van Steen (2019, 229–231). Bond and Craps (2019) discuss the history of trauma and the recent critical debates about the term.

9 The twentieth-century biopolitical dimensions of various European child migration movements have recently been covered in the volume edited by Beatrice Scutaru and Simone Paoli (2021).

10 Van Steen (2019, 49–51).

11 I have been most inspired by the recent trends in life-writing and discovered thought-provoking material and guidance in *New and Experimental Approaches to Writing Lives*, edited by Jo Parnell (2019). I have appreciated its emphasis on alternative forms of life-writing, such as the obituary, but the book does not dwell on the intimate experience of child adoption. The 2003 special issue of *a/b: Auto/Biography Studies* is important, too. The introduction to this special issue, written by Emily Hipchen and Jill Deans (2003) and titled "Adoption Life Writing: Origins and Other Ghosts," led me to Hipchen as series co-editor of *Formations: Adoption, Kinship, and Culture* (OSU Press). Useful, too, has been the most recent book by Margaret Homans (2013), which is devoted to the power and potential of (writing) adoption narratives. Equally important are Honig (2005), Irr (2014), Mcleod (2015), and Novy (2005, 2012, and 2024), and, for a recent practical example, Kim et al. (2018). Notably, however, *FTRWM* does not engage with fictional literature about adoption but focuses on real-life experiences extending into creative nonfiction.

12 The adoptee recipient of the social worker's statement quoted above shared his reaction with me, a couple of days later (source kept confidential). His is the kind of response, however, that he cannot write back to the social worker-expert, on whom he remains dependent for scraps of information from his adoption file:

> It's inexplicably stupid to say such things to an adoptee at any point without knowing the life to which they went and what happened after. But the need to feel good about adoption as fundamentally a sound and nurturing process for so-called unwanted children and infants seems the important element here, not any reality-testing that a little investigation might provide.

13 A Greek pioneer in the genre of "testimony theater" (θέατρο ντοκουμέντο) was Giorgos Michailidis, who staged *Η δίκη των έξ* (*The Trial of the Six*) with his company, the Open Theater, in October of 1974. This "tribunal play" drew from personal testimonies and historical and legal texts (court proceedings) to "perform" the trial of those responsible for the Asia Minor Catastrophe (1919–1922). But Michailidis used the script and the many performances to posit broader questions of responsibility, and especially the responsibility of the world powers, also in the making of the dictatorship and in the loss

of the Greek-Cypriot territories in Northern Cyprus. Spyros Kakouriotis (2022) argues persuasively for the many historical and current layers of Michailidis's production, which revealed influences of Brechtian theater. With Kakouriotis, we may trace the roots of testimony theater back to the politicized theater of the German-speaking world of the 1960s (2022, 95–96) and even earlier, to Erwin Piscator in the 1920s. While the notion of "testimony" tends to prioritize oral sources in English, the Greek term "θέατρο ντοκουμέντο" takes the phrase back to documentary or archival sources. Michailidis incorporated both to great effect, and I have experimented with similar techniques. Zoe Ververopoulou (2023) discusses in detail the "contemporary theater of the real." The scholarship on the genesis of and critical engagement with testimony theater is expanding: see, for instance, Fisher (2020), Hammond and Steward (2012), and Lavender (2024). On the theater of the Greek dictatorship era and the censorship rules of the time, see further Van Steen (2015).

14 I borrow the by now well-worn phrase "adoption triangle" from the title of the pioneering book by Sorosky, Baran, and Pannor (1978).

15 Heijun Wills (2015, 57). Smith and Watson further clarify the term "memoir" by distinguishing it also from autobiography (2010, 1–19, or chapter 1). I concur with them that, "by shifting from *autobiography* and *memoir* to *life writing* and *life narrative*, we suggest the terms in which a new, globalized history of the field might be imagined" (Smith and Watson 2010, 5; italics as in the original).

16 Cardaras included a longer reflection on shifting identity information in Cardaras (2023a in the collective volume 2023b).

17 Eleftheriou, email communication of July 19, 2020.

18 McKee (2019, 120, 124).

19 Mary (South Korean adoptee) (August 1, 2019), "Dear Adoption: I Am Finally Ready to Face You—the Real You, the Darker You." Online at https://dearadoption.com/2017/08/01/dear-adoption-i-am-finally-ready-to-face-you-the-real-you-the-darker-you/.

20 Newton (2022, 3).

21 Bronkhorst and Oost (February 4, 1984): "[D]reigter, even als er een wereldgrondstoffen-en arbeidsmarkt bestaat, een wereldwijde kindermarkt te ontstaan?," 56.

22 For a first experiment with a more direct approach, see Van Steen (July 7, 2018), "'Are We There Yet?' The Greek Adoptees' Road of Return–An Essay." Online at http://ergon.scienzine.com/article/essays/are-we-there-yet.

23 See Rak (2017).

24 I refer to Viviana Zelizer's (1985) seminal work, *Pricing the Priceless Child*.

25 McKee (2019, 10).

26 The third chapter of a recent book by Anita Casavantes Bradford (2022) offers a welcome exception. This chapter, titled "War Orphans and Children on Demand," focuses on the migration of unaccompanied refugee minors and intercountry adoptees between 1945 and 1956 (2022, 70–100).

PART II

FOR THREE REFRIGERATORS AND A WASHING MACHINE: A TESTIMONY THEATER PLAY

INTRODUCTION: VOICINGS OF WHAT CANNOT EASILY BE VOICED

When preparing to go to a stage performance, one does not necessarily go and read the script, let alone any critical analysis. Readers of this play, too, are welcome to go directly to the play, which follows in the next several pages (published below as "Text One"). For them, perhaps a few additional words of introduction are needed. Einstein is claimed to have said, "The secret to creativity is knowing how to hide your sources." This play does the opposite of hiding sources, but that does not mean that it limits creativity. The playscript below offers a selection of authentic texts, whose order can be changed, and whose details can be fleshed out on the stage. The sources tap into lived experiences, and stage performances can bring them back to life. This is why I see the playscript below as a canvas that can be reworked, and why I left a few blank pages for the reader's notes on subsequent versions or animations (solicited here as "Text Two/Too," on p. 65). I owe a huge debt on the original playscript to all known and unknown, incidental authors. I owe an equally large debt to Kyriaki Mitsou, Renata Sofrona, and Romina Spyraki, whom I can thank by name.[1] Like no others, they understood the physical and emotional labor that went into our community-based production process, its demands of organizing and creating momentum, as we prepared for the October 24, 2024, London premiere at the Greenwood Theatre. Also, they chose to center their—reimagined—playscript on the thematic building blocks of "Abandonment" (see book cover image), "Deception," "Searching," and "Discovery" (Figure 3), which worked very well with audiences that were not yet familiar with the history of adoptions from Greece.

FIGURE 3 Searching and occasionally finding. Scene from the premiere production of *For Three Refrigerators and a Washing Machine*, October 24–26, 2024, Greenwood Theatre, London. Photograph by the author.

Belatedly, I invite the reader to the fall 2024 opening production—and to further reading and reimagining—as follows:

Join us for a new and bold play called *For Three Refrigerators and a Washing Machine*, which will make you think differently about the complex history of child adoption and family formation. "Historic" adoptions have been called *the* discussion topic of the current decade, but there is nothing "historic" about these adoptions for those who still live them. Our innovative play sifts through clues and then pieces together the personal story of child adoption that becomes the social history of twentieth-century Greece. For Greece of the 1950s, especially, this is the complex story of the families that were given every chance and those who were given no chance at all.

Thus, *For Three Refrigerators and a Washing Machine* tells the story of international child adoptions from Greece in the 1950s and the 1960s, but this historic adoption movement reveals many points of similarity with subsequent adoptions flows, from Ireland, Korea, China, Central and South America, and elsewhere. The multilingual stage production creates awareness about what has not been said, should be said, but still cannot be said about the losses involved in the permanent uprooting of children. It touches on the difficulties of being sent overseas with a minimum of papers while facing a maximum of expectations. Without any inhibitions, the production asks the thorny question of "At what cost?" and tackles the existential issues of "Where do I come from?" and "What happened to the child I relinquished for adoption abroad?" And why did nobody foresee that adopted children become adopted adults who ask critical questions about origins, procedures, and aftercare?

The enigmatic title *For Three Refrigerators and a Washing Machine* (or in Greek: Για τρία ψυγεία κι ένα πλυντήριο) has its own story to tell: It stems from the fact that the Babies' Center Mitera accepted a donation of three refrigerators and one washing machine from the Netherlands. In exchange for that donation, the Babies' Center agreed to the adoption of 600 Greek children by Dutch parents over the course of some fifteen years. Thus, *FTRWM* covers archives, voices, and rumblings: the files of the cross-border adoptions from postwar Greece and the living testimonies surrounding them.

With the adoptees' contributions, we have been working on an upstream form of "life-written" "testimony theater," which displays affinities with verbatim theater, reminiscence theater, and devised theater.[2] For validating minority perspectives, testimony theater is akin also to history-writing "from below" and to action research and activism. It is not a theater that refuses to put the imagination to work. It is not a passive form of cultural production. To the contrary, the challenge of how to adapt testimony and the textual or visual record to the stage is a different, but no less formidable challenge to the imagination. Also, the performance must integrate the archive of feelings, as they relate to family disruption, child abandonment, loss of language and community, and the arduous endeavor to reconnect with Greek family and culture. Thus, the playscript incorporates notes accompanying Greek foundling children, testimonies from caretakers at orphanages, lawyers' letters, inquiries and replies from prospective parents, internal correspondence from social workers and other intermediaries, the letters of adult adoptees to the author about their desire to search and find, and so on. A quick glance shows that the adoptees' lived experience of international adoption lends itself to modes of dramatization. This multimodal play must act while remaining, at all times, respectful of personal data and private emotions. Meanwhile, the position of readers and spectators is not one of voyeurism, of looking in on the pain of others. Readers and viewers do not remain passive spectators, but become witnesses to a historical and biopolitical phenomenon, which they may previously have passed by silently.

Theater, testimony, archive, and research have blended before in twenty-first-century Greece. A Greek play of 2017, *Το ξύπνημα της Μνήμης. Παιδιά πρόσφυγες του Ελληνικού Εμφυλίου* (*The Awakening of Memory: Child Refugees of the Greek Civil War*) was based on the book *Children of the Greek Civil War: Refugees and the Politics of Memory*, written by Loring Danforth and Riki Van Boeschoten (2012). It foregrounds the experience of war-afflicted children who have grown into adulthood. In a similar fashion, our work fronts the experiences and the stories, painful and otherwise, of some 4,000 Greek-born adoptees who have only recently found their voice, their very own place in what was a massive but forgotten historic adoption movement. This movement deserves the unflattering name of Greece's unrecognized "baby drain." It is associated with the compromising condition of seeing postwar Greek state institutions, lawyers and lawcourts, as well as diaspora organizations involved.[3]

Others, too, have delved into the methods and praxis of testimony theater to tackle painful family and social histories, such as the makers of *Dear Ireland*, which was staged at the Dublin-based Abbey Theatre under pandemic lockdown conditions (2020). The play is a virtual "postcard" sent to Ireland denouncing its fraught history of punitive separations of babies from their unwed mothers.[4] Also, Alan Berks and Leah Cooper have written and directed *In My Heart: The Adoption Play Project*. This 2016 play was "created collaboratively by Wonderlust Productions, the talented cast and crew of the original production and over 200 Minnesotans in the adoption community."[5] The makers of this play, too, understood co-production to be more than just a method: It elevates the ethos that permeates the entire endeavor. In that spirit, they recommend "partnership and collaboration with your local adoption community, both in refining the script to localize it and in performing it," and make themselves available for consultation. We continue to work in shareable performative ways, inspired by all the above, as we promote practices rooted in the extraordinary self-expressive potential of theater and performance. Our play and production urge broad audiences to reflect critically on issues of displacement and permanent identity loss in a Greek, but essentially transferable context—and on the lifelong, taxing efforts to gain back what was lost.

Notes

1 I also value the comments and corrections that Spyros Kakouriotis and Triantafyllos Kotopoulos (2022) shared with me. The references to archival sources, newspaper articles, and other primary sources in this part of the book are given in the notes, for the following three reasons: To preserve confidentiality, some primary source

references remain incomplete and are better contextualized here. Secondly, this system keeps these references directly linked to the main texts and/or quotations in case Part II is reproduced on its own. Thirdly, it further allows me to keep the References section more focused on the pertinent secondary sources and thus more consistent with Part I.

2 See above, p. 15.

3 In fact, if I ever had the option to select a site-specific location to enhance the interpretation of our play, I would choose the old courthouse complex of the Athens Court of First Instance, on Santaroza Street near Omonia Square, with the abandoned book stoa behind it: so much forgotten and neglected history, with hardly a book culture to reflect on it.

4 See https://www.abbeytheatre.ie/dear-ireland/.

5 See https://wlproductions.org/inmyheart/.

FOR THREE REFRIGERATORS AND A WASHING MACHINE

The first postwar adoptions from Greece to the USA served children in need of families. After 1953, the demand for "adoptable" children started to surpass the supply, and intercountry adoption began to cater to families in need of children. Given that American couples had hard currency US dollars on offer, the search for more adoptable children was on. Competition among Greek adoption brokers intensified. Pantelis M. Rozakis, a Greek politician and lawyer, wrote to an American couple, in a letter from 1961:

> I would […] like to advise you—as your lawyer—not to tell that you have already adopted two children, because we will perhaps meet any hesitating by the natural parents. You may only tell that you have not had own children from your marriage and for this reason you want to adopt children of Greece.
>
> […] many Americans […] who had adopted, in the last time [i.e., year, June and July 1960], many, many Greek children from poor and having many children families […] It is […] enough that the natural parents make a solemn [official] abandon act or declaration before a public notary […]. The orphans or foundling children are very rare and not too healthy. Unless this [Otherwise], you will need 2 years, at least, to complete an adoption and you are obliged to bring reports and reports and certificates and certificates from the International Social Organisation [International Social Service], which exige [require] time and time and expenses and expenses and without certitude for an adoption.[1]

The occasional odd twists in Rozakis's language do not hide what is really going on: he is coaching American couples on how to lie and work on the emotions of the birth parents. He is also presenting the easier and more certain solution in the Greek adoption world of the early 1960s: rather than giving a home to a foundling or to a true orphan, he proposes the faster route of persuading existing families to give up one of their children (typically a newborn girl). In his mind, an American couple had more of a right to a new child than a poor Greek couple had to keep its own offspring.

By 1975, some 4,000 Greek children had been dispatched to the USA for adoption, and another 600 were sent to the Netherlands? Why to the Netherlands? Because the Babies' Center Mitera really valued the handsome donation it had received from the Dutch, the three refrigerators and the one washing machine. Six hundred children for three refrigerators and a washing machine.

*****

We humans like to imagine the rides we hitch on stories—obliging plots and accommodating characters that simplify reality—as being like driving our own cars: we can go where we want, and we take for granted having to stay on roads that are already there and obey speed limits and traffic signs. The fearful possibility is that some stories are like amusement park rides—roller coaster rides—that take you where they want, at their speed, and once a decision has been made to get on, the possibilities for getting off are very limited.[2]

*****

Number 900: Ioannis, Sex: male
26/1/1956: date of entry into the Geronymakeio Orphanage
26/1/56 at 11:00 p.m.: the child was received by way of the baby box carrying
   the attached message:

We beg you, please, to keep the newborn child, which was born 9/1/56 and baptized on 10/1/56 with the name of Ioannis. Please do not give him to absolutely anyone, because he is a legitimate child and will later be taken back by his father, given that he lost his mother and his father, who has 6 other children, is unable to raise the infant.

28/5/59: handed over to the International Social Service for adoption in the USA.

Characteristic features:

   Body weight: 3 kilograms
   Hair: brown
   Eyes: azure blue
   Complexion: light like wheat[3]

*****

Newspaper *Atlantis*, Greek Daily Newspaper, New York (Figure 4)

> I beg you to publish who is the American doctor who has taken under his protection […] my children because it is impossible for me to find out where they are and you will oblige me.
>
> Respectfully
>
> George Minouvides
>
> From Gian[n]itsa
>
> 9 years old Siderni [Sideris] Minouvides of George
>
> 7 years old Athanasios Minouvides of George
>
> 3 years old Antonia Minouvides of George

They were taken in Salonica by the AHEPA in the year 1955 and I do not know their fate. I will be very much obliged if you will be able to find out for me where they are. I am a poor farmer and laborer.

FIGURE 4 Searching in New York City. Image from the premiere production of *For Three Refrigerators and a Washing Machine*, October 24–26, 2024, Greenwood Theatre, London. Photograph by the author.

My address is

George Minouvides

Giannitsa

Pellis [Pella], Thessaloniki, Greece[4]

*****

Panagiotis Lentos, director of the Patras Orphanage, to the American adoptive parents of two of his young wards:

> The children that you have chosen, and that we, too, have come to regard as yours, are truly special in every respect. We pray [...] that they may become worthy and honorable citizens. We want them to be true assets as much to their homeland, small but heroic Greece, as to our friend and ally America [...][5]

*****

The American adoptive father declared in a hearing:

> A. Oh, yes, we told him [the middleman] we wanted to adopt the [Greek] children as fast as possible, and he said he would do that for us. He said he would help us to get them here as fast as possible.
>
> Q. Did you tell him what kind of children you wanted?
>
> A. We told him [...] about eighteen months up to two—up to three years, [...] and the only stipulations we said were that we wanted normal healthy children with coloring that would fit into our family, light complected and children that would just fit in with the family group.
>
> [...]
>
> [A]nother thing [...] against the [Greek] boy was that he was very dark complected and it made him hard to fit with the family group.
>
> When I spoke about it to [middleman's name] he said he was sorry, they are our children now and there is nothing he can do about it.[6]

*****

An unhappy mother

entrusts to you

for you to take

the baby born of my flesh,

because, for the time being,

he has no father,

and when I am settled,

I will come and take him back.

I have tied his identification paper

to his little hand, with the name […].

Once again, I beg you,

let him not be lost

or be placed in a stranger's home,

and then I cannot find him anymore.

For all that, thank you[7]

*****

The child is male. He was born

at 10 o'clock in the morning, today

on 5-1-48. He is not baptized.

He comes with the characteristic sign

of a baptismal cross, which has been

tied to his neck with a red thread,

and 4 safety pins attached,

because he is not wearing swaddling straps.[8]

*****

It is not baptized, its little leg

is broken, I have one diaper and one

little blanket for him, the time is 11:30

17-8-67, Thursday, he was born on Wednesday

the 9th of the month.

And may I please ask you to do

a blood test on him.[9]

*****

28 August 1957.

My name is Penelope. I am 15 days old, and I am wearing a little shirt and white pants, and I have with me three white diapers and a little cross. The cross is a token of my baptism.

28 August 2024.

My name is Penelope. The orphanage gave me Odysseos for a last name. I am 67 years old, and I am still waiting, still looking for the person who baptized me and then left me. And what wouldn't I give to have that cross back?![10]

*****

One afternoon, about one month before we gave out baby no. 8422 for adoption, a man came to my ward and asked to see the baby. The man was about 50 years old and shabbily dressed [...]. He told me he was the baby's father. Because the baby was asleep, I opened the door for him, so he could just see it from afar. He cried, and he left two chocolates for me to give to the child later [...]. Then he left. Since then, he has not returned, neither before nor after the child's adoption.[11]

*****

I have been interested in adopting a refugee child for quite a while [...] I am a life-long Unitarian [...] My liabilities are mostly, I think, that I am deaf [...] I tell you this to be honest. I really do not think it would be a handicap with a child; in fact, it may even be an asset in that I think it has aroused my sympathy for others.

As for the child, I would like one of good stock of course and would be doubly pleased if I could get one of an European "peace worker." A girl, preferably under seven years, and even a blond of northern European parentage, if I can get everything I want.[12]

I know you must be very busy but still do I request your very best efforts in my behalf. Failing that, can you pass this on to another party with your whole-hearted recommendation?[13]

*****

I can assure you, your adoption file holds absolutely nothing of interest.[14]

*****

On January 15, 1957, the last group of children processed by the International Social Service under the Refugee Relief Act [of 1953, which expired December 31, 1956] came to New York by plane from Greece. All the children on this flight were for approved families for whom we [the ISS] had suggested the child, except one. The one was a proxy adoption carried out by an adoptive mother from Texas. She was most demanding and irritated that our consultants were not giving her attention and special help. She insisted that she did not have to follow procedure (i.e., immigration) that the other parents did because she had already adopted her child! The consultants who talked with her said she appeared to be drunk, and she appeared to be over 50 years of age. She made the comment at one point that she must be rushed through because she had another baby at home. She also commented that she wished she had adopted all of the babies. Although we realize this child has already been legally adopted, we think that this child may be in need of protection. In fact, it was the feeling of the consultants that this woman was not the type to keep the baby herself and that she may have in mind to give it to someone else.[15]

*****

I have a memory of my mom and 1 walking through the supermarket, and I was holding her up because she was drunk. I was embarrassed because people in the store were looking at us. I wonder now why no one called the police when they saw this [...]. I was about six years old.[16]

*****

Tasoula Vlachou appeared on her own initiative at the Babies' Center Mitera, of whose existence she had heard from a friend of hers, who had given her child for adoption.

Tasoula, aged 18, was born in a village near Thessaloniki and was an orphan from a very tender age. When she was 7, her relatives placed her as a housemaid with a family in Thessaloniki where she remained for several years. She says that this family exploited her [...], later the head of the family corrupted her. Later she met somebody by the name of Michael [...]. She became pregnant from him. She lived with this man for some months; then he left her [...]. Since that date she lived the life of a prostitute. A friend of hers, who was working in a cabaret took her with her, and Tasoula stated various relationships with the clients of this cabaret.

Tasoula gives the impression of having suffered a lot in her life, and she does not trust in the goodness of other people. She wants to go back to Thessaloniki, to the cabaret, make some money, and have a chance to marry someday. She says that many of her girl-friends, after they made some money, married well.

At the Center, Tasoula would not talk with the other mothers, unless they talked to her. With me, she was very talkative, but only to sneer at society and the immorality of those who preach morality. She said that they showed her the road to immorality, and that from now on she intended to look after her own interest, so that she may marry somebody and get out of this hell.

Tasoula gives her baby for adoption gladly. She thinks that a family will give the baby all the love she herself has missed. She asked me to see that the baby goes to a good family.[17]

*****

We think that Pavlos is a very attractive sweet child who would be very easy to find a home for, but it seems most unfortunate that this child, who has a young mother and a family in Greece, should have to be separated from them. The mother is described as easy-going, cheerful, and affectionate, and the crucial problem seems to be that of support for the child. You know well our feeling, which I am sure you share, that it seems most unfortunate for children to be transplanted from their native country when it would seem the best solution to give some kind of economic aid to the child's mother who is most attached to him, so that the painful separation can be avoided.

We look forward to hearing from you as to whether you too think that any solution other than emigration and adoption may not be best in this instance.[18]

*****

"Seinfeld: The Lost Episode," 1995:

In this recently unearthed videotape of the original, rejected pilot for what became the hit NBC series, suburban bakery owners Jerry and Elaine try to keep their marriage fresh by adopting two lovable Greek orphan brothers, George and Cosmo. A warm, plot-driven family comedy. $24.95[19]

*****

Pella, April 26, 1956

Dear Sir,

It is with great emotion that I am parting with my pupil Theodore. But at the same time I am extremely happy because he is leaving our poor town to go to the glorious land of Freedom, which is today the hope of all the Free Nations on the earth.

We are sure that in your civilized country and under your immediate guidance, this child will develop into a useful citizen for the State and yourselves [...]. The good you do is great. We all will be grateful to you.

You will be kind enough to send us a letter from time to time, so we can learn of the child's progress. You cannot imagine how much I, his teacher, will be happy to hear from him.[20]

*****

When my father died, my mother had an emotional breakdown and fell into a deep depression. I was now in the 7th grade and felt alone once again. I did not have a lot of friends and I survived the ordeal by becoming my own best friend. I drew strength from the comfort I gave myself, just like I did when I was in the orphanage. I became somewhat of an introvert and would listen to music, read, and write stories to get through this difficult time.

I took a job babysitting at the age of 13 and at a retail store at the age of 14. This way I would not have to interact with my mother that much. I graduated from high school and attended college, where I really blossomed socially and started to find myself. I entered into an early marriage at the age of 20, and that marriage ended in divorce seven years later. A few years after that divorce, I started dating and eventually married the man I am married to now, my husband of 34 years.

There were other heartaches. I was unable to have children. An attempt to adopt did not move forward due to health issues. I have overcome a lot of challenges since being adopted, but I have remained strong like a willow tree. I bend but I do not break. I believe my adoption and the love I received from my father and my husband have helped make me the strong woman I am today. I have learned how to turn personal trauma into a life full of purpose.[21]

*****

From the *Idaho State Journal*, May 1, 1960, "Child from Greece lauds Mom":

> Ten-year-old Georgia Havens [...] received word that she was an honorable
> mention winner in the mother's essay contest [...]. Georgia's story is an
> interesting one. She came to Pocatello in 1955, at the age of six [...] to be
> adopted by Americans [...]. Georgia couldn't speak any English [...] Now
> she can't recall the Greek words easily.

Here is Georgia's essay which received honorable mention:

> MY MOM IS THE WORLD's BEST BECAUSE [...] She picked me out
> of the orphanage where there were other girls there that she could have
> picked, but she picked me.
>
> I am very happy that I have such a loving mother. She spanked me, but
> she told me that the only reason she did was because she wanted me to grow
> up to be a nice girl. Another reason is because she loves me.

*****

As a young adult, Dad's cruel comments hurt me more than any beating.
One month before my 20th birthday, we had a terrible argument. I don't
remember what we fought about, but the conversation ended when Dad
yelled, "You'd be in some gutter if we hadn't adopted you." I could take it no
more. I turned around, walked away, and moved into an apartment the next
week. I knew Dad felt terrible about his hurtful comment to me, but there
are some things you never say to an adopted child [...] he never apologized.[22]

*****

In the best professional judgment of the two accredited agencies, it is determined
that this couple does not have the capacity for the difficult task of being parents to
an adopted child. However, this is in no sense a reflection on them as individuals
or as citizens in the community.

The local county welfare department was very much concerned when
they learned that the Joneses had mortgaged their property to finance a trip to
Greece to obtain a child. This is especially regrettable in view of their limited

financial assets. The county welfare department offered to talk this matter over with Mr. and Mrs. Jones in an attempt to dissuade them from this major expenditure, but the couple informed them by letter of May 11, 1962, that they did not wish their advice or help.[23]

*****

The Texas support group Parents of Greek Orphans (POGO) lacked "social service concepts and techniques" to secure the best possible placements for its adoptees. It let the petitioners' financial credentials outweigh their moral credentials. Reportedly, the "good Christians" of POGO did insist that each adoptable Greek child be seen by four Greek and one American doctor and that "[t]he child must be free of Negro blood."[24]

*****

My dearest sister,

It is very difficult for me to forget you, the angelic, rosy-cheeked child, who was always happy and at such a young age you used to call my name, "Taki mou." [...] We have never forgotten you. Whenever the family all got together, we always talked about you and your presence was always with us, like you never left.

Your brother Takis[25]

Beloved little sister Yiannoula,

Always good health, that is what I wish for you, too. You cannot imagine the joy that came over me when I learned that you had made great efforts to find out about your parents and your siblings. Many years have passed and the image that comes to my mind is from when you were a baby. I would hold you by the hand and take you out for short walks until our mother would come home from work. You were probably too little to remember me. I think of you a lot and I want to see you and be able to talk to you up close, embrace you, and cry tears of joy together.

Yiannoula, I was worried every single day about when this would happen, after so many difficult years passed. We will finally be able to meet again and talk up close.

Don't ever think I was not thinking of you for all those years that you were gone from me, your brother. When you come, God willing, you will understand how you were being missed. Greece is beautiful. If only you would be able to stay forever, near us, your very own people, your siblings, those who genuinely love you.

When I lost you, however, […] imagine what I went through when I learned that our mother had given you away […] but let me not sadden you any further.

I cannot wait to see you.
With love,
Your brother Christos

*****

"The older we got, the harder it was to adopt a child in this country," said [the adoptive father]. "But we knew we had lived long enough to rear children – so we sidestepped child welfare obstacles in the United States and tried Europe."[26]

*****

We were scheduled to leave [again] for America in a few days. Beatrice [my adoptive mother] told me she realized how much happier I was in the village than in America. She cried saying it, but told me, you don't have to come back with me. Not wanting to lose me now, she had mixed feelings of both anger and sadness. She had no one left and I knew it.

I went and told Stavroula [my birth mother] what she had said. "You are going back to America with your mother. She's old, she won't live long, then you can return," she said. I felt like I belonged in Greece, but I knew I was not wanted. Sadly, I told my mother, Beatrice, that I would be going back to America with her.

On the plane ride home, I had lots of time to reflect on some of the rumors I had heard in the village. I asked Beatrice if they were true; that I was traded for the house that we lived in. She said she didn't know what John had done with the house. I also asked her about my name. She could never pronounce it correctly, so I asked, "Why didn't you just change my name?" She looked at me and said, "I took everything from you. Did you want me to take your name, too?" In my entire life with my mother Beatrice, that was the most profound thing she had ever said to me. I realized then that she knew how I felt.

I know now that the person who truly loved me was Beatrice. She began to look at me with admiration, like I could do anything I set out to do. She thought I was perfect. Even though we had a rough start, she admitted that she did not know how to be a mother. She asked me many, many times for forgiveness, and I did forgive her. She always told me the truth. She was the most honest person I knew, and she thanked me every day of her life for being there for her. And she became the most phenomenal grandmother to my three children.

Beatrice died on November 5, 2009, at the age of 93. I called my mother in Greece to tell her and the only thing she said was, "So, we're all going to die. Did she leave you her money?" I happily told her that there was never any money to be had. But I was so hurt and saddened to realize that Stavroula had sacrificed me, her own child, for financial gain.

Looking back at my adoption, I realize I was a pawn to both sets of parents. Each set had something to gain. I have wondered all these years why my adoption was allowed to happen at all. I was not starving or destitute. Why would they let someone separate a child from her home and family at my age? My parents failed me. The courts failed me. I was a commodity, a bargaining chip.[27]

*****

Internal correspondence among social workers, June 1955:

> The information regarding Zoe was presented to Mr. and Mrs. Smith and they were most receptive of it. They were especially happy that Zoe is a little girl of the right age to become a younger sister to their son, Jonathan. As you could expect, though, they do have some questions.
>
> Has Zoe been seen regularly by a competent doctor?
>
> Could they have the results of a psychological examination of the child, for a more scientific evaluation of her potential?
>
> Although Mr. and Mrs. Smith admit that their heart goes out to Zoe, they realize that they must be somewhat selective because their own son is probably above average. Their chief concern is that the children be happy together, and they feel that this cannot be achieved if a younger child was of less than average ability.
>
> They will wait for further information before making a decision about taking Zoe.

*****

We are in receipt of your letter of May 23rd [1956]. We commented [...] on this [adoption] case previously. Our point is: it is much worse for an average child to be placed with clever people than for a clever child to be placed with average adoptive parents. In view of the fact that we have many more average children, the ones of higher intelligence should be placed with families who have higher intellectual interests. These people undoubtedly have friends of the same level, and their children would play together.

An adopted child has certain problems in any milieu that, if we could avoid the additional striving, we should try. Therefore, we reserve the children of high intelligence for corresponding adoptive parents.[28]

*****

Georgia, the new, ten-year-old arrival from Greece to California, is already observing and taking on American ways. She has stressed, in conversation with her adoptive mother, the need for her dresses to be shortened, to a length just above the knees. Her new mother followed this request, and I noticed that Georgia looked cuter and younger. Perhaps another indication of wanting to be American is that Georgia has realized her skin is dark. She has been scrubbing it to make it white. Her mother has kindly told her that her skin is beautiful and that she need not scrub it this hard.[29]

*****

When my mother was finally located, she was encouraged to see a psychologist, and I was encouraged to find one, too. Information about my own early life was kept from me. And I would be kept from my own mother because an agency that continues to place children across borders thought we couldn't handle it. Time ran out. I found out late last year that my mother died in 2020. I was a year too late. I was her only child.[30]

*****

My beloved daughter,

I cannot believe I found you after all this time. A gap I have been feeling is slowly fulfilled and it will be completely gone when I hold you in my arms. It's like a miracle. Since the day I received your first news I am pleasantly astonished. I don't know from where to start […] The only thing I know is that I can't wait to meet you and hold [you] in my arms […]. Everyone is looking forward to meeting you.

This letter is short but my emotions are endless for you.[31]

*****

New York: Greek orphan M., 10, of Serres, Greece, gets welcoming kisses on arrival here 12/30[/57] via TWA from her new foster mother [...] and her foster brother, Nicholas, Jr., 12. Young Nicholas, also a Greek orphan, arrived in this country in 1954. Mrs [...] said that the girl's name would be changed to Diane, because Nicholas wanted a sister named Diane.[32]

*****

One ignorant Greek mother relinquished her child when a local lawyer told her she would receive $50 a month pension and could rejoin her boy when his education was completed in the U.S. The child was taken; the mother lost track of him. The International Social Service, asked to check, found the mother had signed away her rights and that he had been adopted by a Greek family in New York.[33]

*****

The respondent [Martha Gillies] testified that her husband, knowing that he was suffering from a serious bodily ailment, very much desired, with her concurrence, that after his death she should have a son to depend upon and that it would be well to have one of his nephews come from Greece to this country [USA] and live with them or her for a time so that if he be found a likable, dependable, and altogether desirable person he be adopted here, and that all that either of them attempted to do was to pursue such a course as that, under the stringent immigration laws then in force, Nicholas could be brought to this country for that purpose; that the "consents" which they signed were understood by them to be consents that if Nicholas was given admittance to this country they would adopt him after becoming satisfied that he was suitable for adoption[...].

The foreign adoption has, nevertheless, another angle which prevents its enforcement here. It is in direct conflict with the public policy of this State [New Jersey] in matters of adoption[...]. It is certain that John's wife, Martha, respondent herein, never saw the youth. The young man is a Greek national and has never been in this country. If a letter written by him to the respondent may be interpreted as a fair reflection of his attitude, he is much more intent upon what the assumed relationship may mean to him in money than upon any filial obligation of love, respect or allegiance toward the woman he claims as his foster mother; a state which, grounded in the entire lack of acquaintanceship and of common interests, is not surprising [...].[34]

*****

The Tulsa Tribune (Tulsa, Oklahoma), 17 November 1958:

Seven Children from Greece

Tulsa Grandfather Plays Stork for Six Families

A Tulsa Grandfather played stork today to two of his daughters, three other families here and a family in Virginia.

He is George Petros, 66, [...] a flying grandfather—if there ever was one.

The retired Petros, former Tulsa café owner, flew to Greece six months ago, on a mission to bring back two adopted Greek sons for his one daughter and a daughter for another [...].

Petros arrived in New York Sunday night on a Trans World Airlines flight from Athens [...].

Petros was tired, but explained he had a plane of "captive" babysitters.

Fellow passengers immediately learned of the flying grandfather's mission, and the children were scattered over the plane, with men and women of a half dozen nationalities helping them pass the time.

The little Greeks were rocked to sleep by passengers speaking or humming in a number of languages.

*****

[T]here had to be something fundamentally awry in a society that tried to solve its "illegitimacy problem" by banishing thousands of children to a foreign country, while at the same time doing nothing to address the underlying fears and prejudices that made such banishment both possible and necessary.[35]

*****

In 1966, at the age of 3 or 4, sitting at a kitchen table in Connecticut, I told 3 boys and 2 adults that I wanted my real mommy. Although I can't say exactly why I asked for my mommy that day or why I carried it deep down inside me most of my life, that distant memory would later prove to be very significant.

In 2018, I learned I was adopted, from an early morning email written by the son of his affluent parents who adopted me from an orphanage in Athens, Greece, when I was a baby. He was the oldest of three boys sworn to secrecy by his parents. He obeyed his parents' command until after they both passed away.

Age 54 is the wrong age to tell someone they are adopted. I am a little girl again, asking for my mommy but this time I am crying my eyes out. In 2014, four years before I was told I was adopted, my real mother died of a heart attack. She is survived by her only child. Me.

For the past five years, there is not a day that goes by that I don't think about that tiny little girl at the kitchen table asking for her mommy.

RIP Eleni. RIP Mommy.[36]

*****

The natural parents of this child, being separated, have abandoned their child and are of unknown address. Despite our best efforts, we have not been able to locate them, and they continue to be of unknown address and indifferent to their child.[37]

*****

You cannot imagine what a headache we suffer night and day. All [the waiting parents] are in a state of hyper-nervosity, and they do not have the patience to wait until we call them to tell them the good news. They call us during the day at the office and again at night at home [...] They have set our head spinning (Μᾶς ἔχουν ζαλίσει).[38]

*****

I think about my two fathers. The one who was responsible for my birth was never home, so he barely knew his children and they didn't know him. They received no direction from him to become adults. My adoptive father worked so hard to provide for our little family, and he spent whatever time he could with me.

For this and all that he did, I knew how much he loved me.

It is sad that I never really knew either of my mothers. One could not be part of my life due to distance and circumstance. The other was blinded by her own goals for me, not taking into consideration my thoughts or my own aspirations. Throughout my life, she made every decision for me. There were some good, happy moments, but the most important decisions were colored by the conflict of what each of us wanted for me.[39]

*****

It will help if you can go over […] the following paragraphs which outline what you must do when you receive your child [at the airport].

You will probably want to bring a small gift to welcome your child. Little girls are usually entranced with new dolls […] and with little purses that they can put combs, handkerchiefs and pennies in. The boys like mechanical toys, just as any American child would. It is helpful to have something for each child that will distract and amuse him in the midst of the confusion. Have a nursing bottle and diapers with you if your child is young.[40]

*****

Maria's new mother had also brought her a very lovely child's purse, beautifully hand-sewn, and embroidered white gloves. And the purse contained all the things that a young lady of her age needs: a comb, mirror, fine handkerchief, coin purse, notebook, pencil and pen. Mrs. Ludden has exquisite taste and we all could visualize the joy she will have in dressing up her new daughter.[41]

*****

Jimmy, the adopted boy told his new parents that he wants to stay with them now, or in his own words: "Greece no good. Jimmy stay here." Jimmy has recently talked more about his experiences in Greece, telling of bombs and buildings falling in. His parents are wondering if Jimmy has only heard this told repeatedly or if he did have such experiences. A friend took Jimmy recently to a movie with war action in it, which upset him. Although Jimmy likes the movies very much and asks to go almost every night, he now asks if there is war in it.[42]

*****

My [adoptive] mom thought that I would enjoy eating cherry jello with milk poured over it. She made me sit at the table until I ate it. A match of wills. Finally, after a few hours of sitting at the kitchen table in defiance, I emerged victorious! And mom? She had to clean a nauseating bowl of pink liquid. I was six.[43]

*****

[Mr Peterson] here in Ethiopia has informed us that it would be wise to contact you concerning adopting children from Greece. We are labouring for the Lord here in the land of Ethiopia under the Sudan Interior Mission. We have been married for 10 years but have no children. There are many Greek merchants in this part of the world and the Lord has laid it on our hearts to consider adopting children from Greece. We feel now is the time to adopt because we are of an age to really enjoy having children. Our ages are […] 34, and […] 37.

We are looking onto the Lord, and, in writing to you, we are taking a step in the right direction. We would appreciate any help that you could give us. We are an American couple.

In His Name

Mr and Mrs Smith[44]

*****

The only question they [the Greek judges] asked Fred was how much money he made. He answered in English, and it was translated into Greek drachmas. There was a gasp from the few spectators in the room. Obviously, we were considered affluent and whatever faults we might have disappeared with Fred's answer. In a few more minutes the hearing was over and we were declared […] the parents of the illegitimate, unbaptized child of Anastasia Papadopoulou. It was over and we were now parents. It was so anticlimactic.[45]

*****

I waited nervously for the searcher's response while I shifted in my seat in the kitchen, readying the pen and adjusting the paper in front of me. I'll need to physically record my past. I'll need to actually look at it, and read it over and over and over again.

"Yes, of course. Well, we know your mother's name, we know your father's name, and we found out something incredible." In that brief moment when she paused, before she continued, I thought to myself, nothing can be more incredible than what I've just been told.

I had no idea just how wrong I was.

Being adopted, or to be more accurate, given up, means expendable. Not on a conscious level, but deep inside that private place we all have where we muster the courage to face the world, where we define ourselves in the most fundamental way. You do not measure up and never quite arrive. It is a picture that is always distorted, at times dramatically, at other times just somewhat, but never completely clear, never totally right. You are different. You just are.

"You have a twin brother," Eleni said. I looked at the phone for a moment, not processing what I've just heard. "I have a what?" She repeated herself. "You have a twin brother."

Twin. Brother.

I wrote down those two words and as my wife read them, I saw her eyes widen. I was suddenly afraid she was going to faint. If I wasn't sitting, I was afraid of the exact same thing.

"He is a priest in the suburbs of Athens. You are not exact. He has blond hair and blue eyes," Eleni gently explained.

I was staring at the paper in front of me and I could not believe what I was seeing. A fraternal twin brother. A Greek Orthodox priest, a full sibling, who has lived out the past 40 years in a life that I've known nothing about. As I struggled as a 10-year-old, a 15-year-old, a 20-year-old, so did he. Somehow, we were separated and wound up in different orphanages, the details of which remain unclear. My twin was ultimately adopted by a family in Greece, and me by a family in the United States.

How can this possibly be real? I found myself thinking that these things only happen in dreams, and they certainly don't happen to me.[46]

*****

Good morning, Helen,

Thank you for the pictures and the document from 1961. What you have there is a list of expenses related to your keep by your great-aunt, and to be shown to your adoptive parents, so they could cover the cost.

It starts by saying: I received $600, that is 17,910 drachmas

Patriotic Foundation [this is PIKPA] 450

Visa 750

Passport 250

Lawyer 6,000

Doctor 1,000

Medicines and milk Nutricia 1,150

Clothing items 2,000

Cost to the wetnurse 3,500

Transportation costs 1,200

Doctor of the US Consulate 200

To the mother of the little one: pictures and letter-writing 700

For the room and board of Elenitsa 2,000

Telegram 100

The total comes to 19,300, so one has to presume that your parents made sure to cover the difference.

The most expensive item is the lawyer, which does not surprise us.[47]

*****

In mid-July 1971, my mother left me at the Church of Saint George Karytsis, in the center of Athens. According to the caretaker, she sat with me in the church for some two hours. She was young, around 18 or so, and tall.

She had me dressed in beautiful clothes and she wrote on a note that I was not baptized.

She left 100 drachmas in the baby basket.

If anyone knows anything, please inform me, so that I can find her.[48]

*****

Dear Gonda,

I have had these documents my whole life and in just a few hours, YOU have answered the question of my birth mother.

So, how ironic that on the eve of my birthday, I should find out her name. I assume that since she was not married that is the reason for not having my birth father's name. It must have been so difficult for these young mothers to have to give up their children just because of societal pressure and stigma. It was quite sad and unfair. My heart goes out to all of these strong women. A question, since I have a Greek birth certificate, am I eligible to obtain Greek citizenship? (Figure 5)

What are our steps moving forward with respect to finding my birth mother? If we cannot find her, I assume that there will not be any way of tracking down my birth father? Just the thought that there is really a possibility of finding her has not yet set in. I'm sitting here and still find it hard to believe that my simple email to you 2 months ago has brought me here.

As I have said before, no matter what does happen or not happen, I thank you from the bottom of my heart.

Sincerely,

Edward[49]

FIGURE 5 Maria's Greek identity reintegrated. Image from the scene titled "Discovery," from the premiere production of *For Three Refrigerators and a Washing Machine*, October 24–26, 2024, Greenwood Theatre, London. The image of the Greek passport page is from the personal archive of Maria Heckinger, with permission. Photograph by the author.

*****

In 2017, while searching the internet, I found a Facebook group that was dedicated to Greek orphans. I found out I wasn't the only one in my situation. I found other people like me, who quickly became friends. I was encouraged to take additional DNA tests and to upload them to other websites so that I could be represented on several different databases. Currently, I am on seven of them. I have been in contact with seven distant cousins, two in Australia and five in the United States. I continue to get new DNA matches, but no relatives who are really close matches.[50]

*****

In February or March 1966, I was adopted by a Dutch couple from the Babies' Center Mitera. I was able to visit Mitera a couple of times [...] I had plans to come to Athens often to have a sense of the country of my birth, to feel and smell it, to experience what it was like to live there. I also intended to find out about my biological family, my background, my history.

Sadly, my life took a different turn. I am now a disabled person suffering from anxiety disorder and rheumatic arthritis, and it is no longer possible to travel to Greece. I find this difficult to cope with. It causes me much heartache and deep sadness that it has become impossible to visit my motherland.

In the past Mitera has assisted me in my search for my biological family. Unfortunately, this did not yield much result. Mitera advised me that I could not meet my biological mother, since her situation was very complex. I am deeply sorry that I never had the opportunity to meet her. Later I was told that she had passed away.

The last information I received from Mitera is that my entire family has passed away. Even today I find this very difficult to accept. Is there really no family member that is alive?

This question occupies my mind. It plays a huge role in my life. I am sure you will understand that I feel this lack, this emptiness and loss, deeply. I find it hard to reconcile myself to the idea that I will never know the circumstances of my birth, that I will never meet my biological family, or even see pictures of them.

I carry my roots in my body and in my soul, even more so now as I am getting a little older. This is why I am [turning] to you.[51]

This latter dated January 29, 2020, has not received a response to this day.

*****

Suggestions for Musical Accompaniments

In English:

—"Dance with Me: Let's dance, little stranger, show me secret sins," by Nouvelle Vague (https://www.youtube.com/watch?v=xqdYqIYNiZM).
—"Love Child," by Diana Ross and the Supremes (https://www.youtube.com/watch?v=hIwdyIpmg-I).
—"Lucky Girl," song by Ulrika Skogby, Greek-born adoptee sent to Sweden (released July 2023: https://www.youtube.com/watch?v=qd80Z3MpiZc).
—"Lullaby in Blue," by Bette Midler (from "Wind beneath Your Wings") (https://www.youtube.com/watch?v=an3e-3xSXKk).

In Greek:

—"*Kalinychta Kemal*" (Nikos Gkatsos—Manos Chatzidakis).
—"Μάνα μου Ελλάς: Τα ψεύτικα τα λόγια τα μεγάλα" (Nikos Gkatsos—Stavros Xarchakos, from the soundtrack of the film *Rebetiko* by Kostas Ferris).

—"Μητέρα, φίλη μου παλιά" (Charis Alexiou, https://www.youtube.com/watch?v=
L4XzbjdSMik).

—"Χωρίς να σ' έχω" (Manolis Lidakis—Vaso Allagianni, https://www.youtube.com/
watch?v=P9_P8fRip9Y).

—"Τον εαυτό του παιδί απ' το χέρι κρατάει" (Marios Frangoulis—Paraskevas Karasoulos,
https://www.youtube.com/watch?v=BX3Ztxtm6F4).

—"Tzivaeri," traditional Greek song.

Notes

1 Letter from the personal archive of Greek-born adoptee T.P. I use only pseudonyms
   or initials, unless the adoptees themselves insist that I use their real names.
2 Quoted from Arthur Frank (2010, 151).
3 Letter from the archive pertaining to Greek-born adoptee E.L. The name Ioannis is
   fictitious, as is his admission number.
4 Letter mailed from Greece on 4 November 1959 and received and translated by the
   Greek American paper *Atlantis* on 10 December 1959. Quoted and contextualized
   by Van Steen (2019, 219).
5 Letter dated 23 July 1954 and currently held in the personal archive of Pam. See Van
   Steen (2019, 183).
6 Quoted from the court proceedings on a case related to the case of Greek adoption
   broker Stephen Scopas (late 1950s–early 1960s).
7 Note accompanying foundling child, which was delivered to the Patras Orphanage,
   without date. The originals of this and the following notes reveal a fair number of
   spelling mistakes, which may indicate that the person who delivered the baby had
   received only a basic education.
8 Note accompanying foundling boy, who was delivered to the Patras Orphanage in 1948.
9 Note accompanying foundling boy, who was delivered to the Patras Orphanage in 1967.
10 Note accompanying foundling girl, who was delivered to the Patras Orphanage in
   1957. Accompanied by her comment later in life.
11 Nurse Katerina Tambakidou, a staff member at the Saint Stylianos Foundling Home, is
   quoted by Kaiti Daravinga (January 9, 1963), "Πόρισμα ενόρκου διοικητικής ανακρίσεως,"
   "Findings of the Administrative Interrogation under Oath," p. 6. Typescript report, 10
   pages, held in the Historical Archive of Macedonia, Records of the court case of the Saint
   Stylianos Foundling Home (GRGSA-IAM JUS 008.02) (Thessaloniki).
12 Letter dated 22 February 1942, see https://iiif.lib.harvard.edu/manifests/view/
   drs:12717158$1i in Box 1, Folder 3, of the archives of the Unitarian Service Committee,
   Administrative Records, 1946–1950, bMS16029. The archives are held at the Andover-
   Harvard Theological Library, Harvard Divinity School, Cambridge, MA.
13 See https://iiif.lib.harvard.edu/manifests/view/drs:12717158$30i and https://iiif.
   lib.harvard.edu/manifests/view/drs:12717158$31i. This letter does not place the
   prospective mother in a positive light, and I keep her name confidential. However, it
   was not at all unusual for hopeful adopters to state their age, sex, and ethnic/racial
   preferences when inquiring about the availability of children in Europe. In the years
   following, the adoption mediators attached pictures of the available children to their
   files, to help answer precisely such questions before they were even spoken.

14 Words spoken by the PIKPA archivist to Greek-born adoptee Mary Cardaras, in a private meeting on June 30, 2022.
15 Letter dated 8 February 1957 and written by Susan T. Pettiss to Rosalind Giles, who served as director of the Child Welfare Division of the state of Texas. The letter is held in the archives of the International Social Service, American Branch Papers, box 10, folder 3: "Adoption 1955–1958," Social Welfare History Archives, University of Minnesota Libraries (Minneapolis, MN).
16 Confidential testimony given by a Greek-born adoptee, July 30, 2017.
17 Social history of a Greek birth mother, compiled by an adoption case worker in 1958–1959.
18 Letter dated March 13, 1956, from the archive pertaining to Greek-born adoptee L.K. The letter was directed to colleagues within the same adoption service.
19 Anonymous, "Seinfeld: The Lost Episode," *Chicago Tribune*, December 15, 1995.
20 Letter from the personal archive of Greek-born adoptee M.B.
21 Greek-born adoptee Fran, personal testimony, September 29, 2019.
22 Maria Heckinger (2019, 101).
23 Letter dated August 13, 1962, held in the personal archive of K.R.
24 Valdemar Gonzales (July 27, 1960), "A Report on The Association of Parents of Greek Orphans," p. 2. Typescript, 6 pages, held in the archives of the International Social Service, American Branch Papers, box 10, folder 18: "Independent Adoption Schemes: Diavitis [*sic*], Reverend Spyrus 1960," Social Welfare History Archives, University of Minnesota Libraries (Minneapolis, MN). Quoted and contextualized by Van Steen (2019, 178–179).
25 This and the following little letter were received by Robyn from her full sibling brothers in 2008. Robyn discusses this letter in her very personal contribution to the collective volume of Greek-born adoptee testimonies, titled *Voices of the Lost Children of Greece: Oral Histories of Cold War International Adoption*, edited by Mary Cardaras (2023b, 127).
26 Anonymous, *The Amarillo Globe-Times* (Amarillo, Texas), June 29, 1960.
27 Chris in Cardaras (2023b, 107–108).
28 Letter dated May 29, 1956, from the archive pertaining to Greek-born adoptee P.M.
29 Letter dated April 6, 1956, from the archive pertaining to Greek-born adoptee M.D.
30 Greek-born adoptee Mary Cardaras, personal testimony, made available online on 27 February 2022: https://youtu.be/ApPboMlswkA.
31 Letter from the personal archive of Greek-born adoptee L.H.
32 UP Telephoto caption, December 30, 1957.
33 Cynthia Lowry (1958), "Mail Order Babies Wanted: Hundreds of Foreign Children Adopted by Proxy," *Democrat and Chronicle* (Rochester, New York), March 9, 1958, p. 11.
34 Matter of Estate of Gillies, 83 A. 2d 889—NJ: Supreme Court 1951.
35 Mike Milotte, writing about the Irish-to-American adoption transports of illegitimate babies, in *Banished Babies: The Secret History of Ireland's Baby Export Business* (2012, 17).
36 Greek-born adoptee, confidential testimony, December 4, 2022.
37 Lawyer's English translation of a Greek document related to an adoption from the Kalamata Orphanage, kept confidential at the request of the archive holders.

38 Quoted from letters dated August 28, 1958 and January 19, 1959, found in a Greek lawyer's records. Names kept confidential.
39 Charlie in Cardaras (2023b, 67).
40 Instructions issued by the International Social Service in 1956, meant to prepare American adoptive parents for the first meeting with their adoptive children at the airport in New York.
41 Letter from the personal archive of Greek-born adoptee M.A.
42 Letter from the personal archive of Greek-born adoptee B.B.
43 Greek-born adoptee P.S., personal testimony posted on Facebook, July 10, 2020.
44 Letter from the late 1950s, found in a Greek lawyer's records.
45 Naomi Moessinger (2003, 41–42). The birth mother's name has been altered.
46 Robert in Cardaras (2023b, 55).
47 Van Steen, email exchange with H.T., December 8, 2022.
48 Leda K., on Facebook, November 5, 2023.
49 Edward, email exchange with the author, March 26, 2023.
50 Nick in Cardaras (2023b, 120).
51 Letter written by Greek-born adoptee E.A. to the Babies' Center Mitera.

TEXT TWO/TOO

REFERENCES

Alvarado, Jules (2020). "Foreword." In *Rooted in Adoption: A Collection of Adoptee Reflections*, edited by Veronica Breaux and Shelby Kilgore. Florida: n.p.

Atta, Dean (2019). *The Black Flamingo*. London: Hodder.

Berks, Alan, and Leah Cooper, dir. (2016). *In My Heart: The Adoption Play Project*. Wonderlust Productions (https://wlproductions.org/inmyheart/).

Bertocci, Doris, Christopher F. Deeg, and Linda Mayers, eds. (2024). *Handbook on the Clinical Treatment of Adopted Adolescents and Young Adults*. New York: Routledge.

Bond, Lucy, and Stef Craps (2019). *Trauma*. London and New York: Routledge.

Bronkhorst, M., and J. Oost (February 4, 1984). "Kinderen op bestelling? Problemen rond interlandelijke adoptie." (Translation: Children on Order? Problems Surrounding Intercountry Adoption). *Algemeen Politieblad* 3: 51–57.

Cardaras, Mary (2023a). "Time Run Out." In *Voices of the Lost Children of Greece: Oral Histories of Cold War International Adoption* (pp. 163–177). London and New York: Anthem Press.

Cardaras, Mary, ed. (2023b). *Voices of the Lost Children of Greece: Oral Histories of Cold War International Adoption*. London and New York: Anthem Press. (Greek translation: *Φωνές των χαμένων παιδιών της Ελλάδας: Μαρτυρίες υιοθεσιών την εποχή του Ψυχρού Πολέμου*, translator: Myrto-Zoe Rigopoulou. Athens: Potamos, 2023).

Casavantes Bradford, Anita (2022). *Suffer the Little Children: Child Migration and the Geopolitics of Compassion in the United States*. Chapel Hill, NC: The University of North Carolina Press.

Danforth, Loring M., and Riki Van Boeschoten (2012). *Children of the Greek Civil War: Refugees and the Politics of Memory*. Chicago: University of Chicago Press.

Didion, Joan (2011). *Blue Nights*. New York: Alfred A. Knopf.

Eleftheriou, Joanna (2020). *This Way Back*. Morgantown, WV: West Virginia University Press.

Fisher, Amanda Stuart (2020). *Performing the Testimonial: Rethinking Verbatim Dramaturgies*. Manchester: Manchester University Press.

Frank, Arthur W. (2010). *Letting Stories Breathe: A Socio-Narratology*. Chicago and London: The University of Chicago Press.

Glaser, Gabrielle (2021). *American Baby: A Mother, a Child, and the Shadow History of Adoption*. New York: Viking.

Hammond, Will, and Dan Steward, eds. (2012). *Verbatim, Verbatim: Contemporary Documentary Theatre*. London: Bloomsbury.

Heckinger, Maria (2019). *Beyond the Third Door: Based on a True Story*. Vancouver, WA: n.p.

Heijun Wills, Jenny (2015). "Fictional and Fragmented Truths in Korean Adoptee Life Writing." *Asian American Literature: Discourses and Pedagogies* 6: 45–59.

Hipchen, Emily, and Jill Deans (2003). "Introduction: Adoption Life Writing: Origins and Other Ghosts." *a/b: Auto/Biography Studies* 18 (2): 163–170.

Homans, Margaret (2013). *The Imprint of Another Life: Adoption Narratives and Human Possibility*. Ann Arbor: University of Michigan Press.

Honig, Elizabeth Alice (2005). "Phantom Lives, Narratives of Possibility." In *Cultures of Transnational Adoption*, edited by Toby Alice Volkman (pp. 213–222). Durham, NC: Duke University Press.

Irr, Caren (2014). "Literature and Adoption: Themes, Theses, Questions." *American Literary History* 26 (2): 385–395.

Kakouriotis, Spyros (2022). *"Η δίκη των έξ, μια παράσταση της Μεταπολίτευσης: Από τη Μικρασιατική Καταστροφή στην εισβολή στην Κύπρο."* (Translation: *"The Trial of the Six*, a Production of the Redemocratization Period: From the Asia Minor Catastrophe to the Invasion of Cyprus"). *ArcheioTaxio* 24: 89–98.

Kim, Cerrissa, Katherine Kim, Sora Kim-Russell, and Mary Kim-Arnold, eds. (2018). *Mixed Korean: Our Stories. An Anthology*. Bloomfield, IN: Truepenny Publishing.

Lavender, Andy (2024). *Documentary Theatre and Performance*. London: Bloomsbury.

Lowry, Cynthia (March 9, 1958). "Mail Order Babies Wanted: Hundreds of Foreign Children Adopted by Proxy." *Democrat and Chronicle*. Rochester, New York, p. 11.

Lynch, Gordon (2016). *Remembering Child Migration: Faith, Nation-Building and the Wounds of Charity*. London and New York: Bloomsbury.

Lynch, Gordon (2020). "Catholic Child Migration Schemes from the United Kingdom to Australia: Systemic Failures and Religious Legitimation." *Journal of Religious History* 44 (3): 273–294.

Mary (South Korean adoptee) (August 1, 2019). "Dear Adoption: I Am Finally Ready to Face You—the Real You, the Darker You." https://dearadoption.com/2017/08/01/dear-adoption-i-am-finally-ready-to-face-you-the-real-you-the-darker-you/.

Mazower, Mark (2017). *What You Did Not Tell: A Russian Past and the Journey Home*. New York: Other Press.

McKee, Kimberly D. (2019). *Disrupting Kinship: Transnational Politics of Korean Adoption in the United States*. Urbana, IL: University of Illinois Press.

McLeod, John (2015). *Life Lines: Writing Transcultural Adoption*. London: Bloomsbury.

Milotte, Mike (2012) [first edition 1997]. *Banished Babies: The Secret History of Ireland's Baby Export Business*. Dublin: New Island Books.

Moessinger, Naomi (2003). "From Couple to Family." In *Welcome Home! An International and Nontraditional Adoption Reader*, edited by Lita Linzer Schwartz and Florence W. Kaslow (pp. 35–50). Binghamton, NY: Haworth Clinical Practice Press.

Newton, Grace (2022). "The Trauma and Healing of Consciousness." *Child Abuse & Neglect* 130, pt. 2. https://doi.org/10.1016/j.chiabu.2022.105563.

Novy, Marianne (2005). *Reading Adoption: Family and Difference in Fiction and Drama*. Ann Arbor: University of Michigan Press.

Novy, Marianne (2012). "New Territory: Memoirs of Meeting Original Family by Seven Adopted American Women." *Adoption & Culture* 3: 124–140.

Novy, Marianne (2024). *Adoption Memoirs: Inside Stories.* Philadelphia: Temple University Press.

Parnell, Jo, ed. (2019). *New and Experimental Approaches to Writing Lives.* London: Macmillan/Red Globe Press.

Pipyrou, Stavroula (2020). "Displaced Children, Silence, and the Violence of Humanitarianism in Cold War Italy." *Anthropological Quarterly* 93 (3): 429–459.

Rak, Julie (2017). "Radical Connections: Genealogy, Small Lives, Big Data." *a/b: Auto/Biography Studies* 32 (3): 479–497.

Scutaru, Beatrice, and Simone Paoli, eds. (2021). *Child Migration and Biopolitics: Old and New Experiences in Europe.* London and New York: Routledge.

Smith, Sidonie, and Julia Watson (2010) [first edition 2001]. *Reading Autobiography: A Guide for Interpreting Life Narratives.* Minneapolis, MN and London: University of Minnesota Press.

Sorosky, Arthur D., Annette Baran, and Reuben Pannor (1978). *The Adoption Triangle: The Effects of the Sealed Record on Adoptees, Birth Parents, and Adoptive Parents.* Garden City, NY: Anchor Press / Doubleday.

The United Nations Refugee Agency (UNHCR) (2021). *2021 UNHCR Best Interests Procedure Guidelines: Assessing and Determining the Best Interests of the Child.* Geneva, Switzerland: United Nations High Commissioner for Refugees.

Ticktin, Miriam (2011). *Casualties of Care: Immigration and the Politics of Humanitarianism in France.* Berkeley, Los Angeles, and London: University of California Press.

Van der Kolk, Bessel (2014). *The Body Keeps the Score: Brain, Mind, and Body in the Healing of Trauma.* New York: Viking.

Van Steen, Gonda (2015). *Stage of Emergency: Theater and Public Performance under the Greek Military Dictatorship of 1967–1974.* Oxford: Oxford University Press.

Van Steen, Gonda (July 7, 2018). "'Are We There Yet?' The Greek Adoptees' Road of Return–An Essay." In *Ergon: Greek/American Arts and Letters,* edited by Yiorgos Anagnostou. http://ergon.scienzine.com/article/essays/are-we-there-yet.

Van Steen, Gonda (2019). *Adoption, Memory, and Cold War Greece: Kid pro quo?* Ann Arbor: University of Michigan Press. (Greek translation: *Ζητούνται παιδιά από την Ελλάδα: Υιοθεσίες στην Αμερική του Ψυχρού Πολέμου,* translator: Ariadni Loukakou. Athens: Potamos, 2021).

Van Steen, Gonda (2021). "Of Foundlings and 'Lostlings': When the Scopas Scandal Rocked the Unstable Foundations of the First 1950s Intercountry Adoptions." *Annales de démographie historique,* special issue on the history of adoption, "Formes adoptives (XVIe–XXe siècles)," 141 (1): 123–155.

Verrier, Nancy Newton (2012) [first edition 1993]. *The Primal Wound: Understanding the Adopted Child.* Baltimore, MD: Gateway Press.

Ververopoulou, Zoe (2023). *Το σύγχρονο θέατρο του πραγματικού: Από τις αληθινές ιστορίες στο θέατρο-ντοκουμέντο και στις ερευνητικές δραματουργίες του 21ου αιώνα.* (Translation: *The Contemporary Theater of the Real: From True Stories to Documentary Theater and to the Research-based Stage Productions of the 21st Century).* Athens: Papazisis.

Zelizer, Viviana A. (1985). *Pricing the Priceless Child: The Changing Social Value of Children.* New York: Basic Books.

INDEX